Practical Strengths:
A CliftonStrengths® Guide for Everyday Ways

Communication Styles

By Jo Self

Practical Strengths
A CliftonStrengths® Guide for Everyday Ways

Communication Styles

By Jo Self

2023

Content Editor
Holly Magnuson

Foreword by
Jennifer Doyle Vancil, M.Ed.

http:/discoverjoself.com
Copyright 2023 by Jo Self
Terms and Nomenclature Licensed from Gallup®

**For my son, O
who continually inspires me to build a
Strengths-Based Generation**

I also hold the deepest gratitude for:

Jennifer

For your continued support and encouragement

Holly

For stepping up and making sure this book made it to the
light of day

Jennifer M and Mary Sue I

Who graciously shared their original documents which
inspired this book

Samir

For introducing me to the world of strengths

And finally, *Dr. Donald Clifton*, thank you for your vision
and belief in seeing what is right in people

And to *everyone* who shared their stories
and gave this book their personal touch!

CONTENT

Why Communication

There is a misconception that those with the talent theme of Communication® are the only people who can communicate well. As someone who has Communication® in her top 5, I can promise you, the words don't always flow. In fact, many years ago I was working with the communications department of a large organization and not one of them had Communication in their top 5 (at that time we didn't have access to all 34). This flustered them greatly until we worked through how other talents were leading to their success.

The beauty of CliftonStrengths® is that each talent theme has its own little glossary. This consists of:

- I am…
- I do…
- I contribute…
- I need…
- I value…
- I'm bothered by…
- And a barrier label (the darker side of the talent)

This basic understanding of each talent theme contributes to a deeper understanding of the intrinsic motivations and needs of each person, which ultimately impacts how we communicate – and how we need to be communicated to. For me, our talents give a glimpse into our own love language.

I believe we need to trust that most people lead with positive intention, including through what and how they are trying to communicate. However, in times of stress or difficulty, we often don't show up at our best, and that can lead to conflict and misunderstandings.

My goal, throughout this book, is to shed some light on how our strengths impact our own communication style. It's how we might see others through a less judgmental lens by understanding their style as well. It's about being conscious and creating deeper connections.

Communication is about more than what we say. We need to consider other questions like: Do they think in the moment or do they need time to process? Do they prefer written or verbal communication? How can we interpret their body language based on what we know about their strengths?

This isn't necessarily about changing how we communicate but recognizing the impact of what we say and how we say it. It's what questions to ask and what behaviors or actions can we introduce in order to open the channels of communication so we can truly hear one another. To no longer assume someone's underlying motivations, but to recognize them.

I highly recommend you review the next section, *"How to Use this Book"* in order to get the most out of the information and advice which has been shared. Should you like to access the resources associated with this book, please visit http://discoverjoself.com/resources. By clicking that link (or copying it) you can download the tipsheet with the brief contribution definitions for each talent.

Why CliftonStrengths®?

I BELIEVE STRENGTHS ARE THE SHORT CUT GLOSSARY
INTO THE HUMAN PSYCHE THAT ALLOWS US TO BUILD
BETTER RELATIONSHIPS
THROUGH BETTER COMMUNICATION
AND GREATER COMPASSION.

It is *'why'* we are and *why* we are here.

@discoverjoself
http:/discoverjoself.com
On a mission to teach
Strengths as a 2nd language

4

Talents are naturally recurring patterns of thought, feeling, or behavior that can be productively applied.

A strength is the ability to consistently provide near-perfect performance in a specific activity.

Talents, knowledge, and skills - along with the time spent practicing, developing your skills, and building your knowledge base - combine to create your strengths.

- Gallup®

Foreword

As long as I've known Jo Self, I've seen that helping people understand how strengths affect their communication is a driver for her. Her "Language of You" program helps people define their personal brand and not only understand who they are, but value it as well. For those who want to embrace the language of Strengths more profoundly, she offers her, "Strengths as a 2nd Language" course. Her one on one "Talent Detangler" service helps people get clear on how to articulate their strengths in writing, and her Facebook group is called "Speaking of Strengths."

As a person driven with Communication in her own top 5, she's passionate about helping people communicate effectively. She does this through her work as a corporate trainer, as a curriculum designer, in her marketing work, and as the passionate author of this Practical Strengths book series.

I'd venture to say that this Communication Styles book is her favorite so far as it captures how strengths affect our interactions with others and helps us understand all the nuances of communication. This includes how we might even frustrate others with our communication styles. Looking individually at each of the 34 talent themes from the CliftonStrengths® assessment, this book advises us all on how to communicate more effectively.

Having collaborated with Jo as a colleague, I've frequently seen her deep commitment to helping people communicate by understanding their strengths. She knows it so well it seeps into her every conversation. She says things like "My Command is deciding the book will be published by this date," and "My Activator is leading here and I am asking each person to follow this structure in their submission."

Once when she was traveling and her plans changed, I immediately asked her "What is the gift here?" She replied, "Does your Positivity always jump in so quickly? Don't I get even a moment to lament the change of plans?" We both laughed out loud at how much strengths language seeps into our conversations.

It is her absolute lens on the world, and her passion is that others can join her in seeing the world through that same lens of strengths. As most of us who have heard Jo speak or read her other books know, her enthusiasm is contagious.

I believe that at the heart of Jo's strong commitment to helping people communicate more effectively is a deep desire to change the world. It's so obvious to her how people's strengths drive their every interaction that she spots it naturally.

This book is her attempt to share that with the world - to help others see what she sees, hear what she hears, notice what she notices. And the advice she's included for understanding and connecting with people who have each strength is her gift to us all.

People of every Strengths profile will find value in understanding their own strengths better, what to celebrate about them, and how they sound to others. They will also gain a valuable understanding of others and learn how others' strengths play into the way they communicate. And how, if they really seek to understand, they can see the intention in the communication styles of others and not just what frustrates them.

This book has the potential to change the way people in all kinds of relationships communicate. Managers and consultants can use this book to help workplace teams understand each other and communicate better. Coaches can use the information in this book to help individuals gain self-knowledge as well as knowledge of those around them and take action to be more effective in every interaction. Educators can help students learning about communication to understand the impact of natural talents on communication styles. The potential value is far-reaching, and I'm grateful for Jo's commitment to writing this book, the third in her Practical Strengths series.

I've been honored to leverage my own Communication talents to contribute an anecdote to each of Jo's Practical Strengths books and to collaborate with her on the overall structure of this Communication Styles book and the content of the Career Success book. And in that collaboration, I've learned that Jo Self is a person so deeply committed to sharing the practical value of strengths that she is devoting her life to it. That commitment led to the writing of this book, and because she did, we'll all be able to communicate better.

Jennifer Doyle Vancil, M.Ed.
Communication Connectedness Maximizer Woo Relator Positivity Belief
Owner of Communicating Strengths LLC
http://communicatingstrengths.com

Introduction

I fell in love with CliftonStrengths® way back in 2003. I was introduced to it when it was still known as StrengthsFinder® by a dear friend, Samir Gupte. The moment I learned my top five talents, I was hooked. It was as if I had received a user's manual for myself! The words that had always failed me when describing why I did, or what I did, or enjoyed something so much were now laid out before me. It was life changing.

Over the years, whenever someone came to me for advice, the first thing I would ask was, "do you know your strengths?" I would immediately have them read, *Now, Discover Your Strengths*, and then have them come back to me. Knowing their top five allowed me to have a deeper understanding of who they were and who they had the potential to be. Eventually this passion led me to become one of the first Spanish-speaking Gallup® Certified Strengths coaches in 2015. It is not just a job - it's a calling.

When people ask me, "Why Strengths?" My answer is fairly simple. I believe that our strengths are the short-cut glossary into the human psyche that allows us to build better relationships through better communication and greater compassion. At the end of the day, it's *why* we are and *why* we're here. I truly believe if we can just appreciate the depth of understanding these 34 talents can give us, we can improve our relationships immensely - from the most intimate to the community-at-large. Once you see yourself objectively, you have no choice but to do the same for others as well. It allows us grace with ourselves, and others, that we may not have otherwise.

While there are some amazing materials out there to help us understand our talents at a deeper level, I always felt there was a small piece missing. Much of what exists is helpful in the professional realm, but there was a void in the day-to-day use of our talents - and our talents are *always* with us. They may show up differently in our different roles (parent, sibling, employee, volunteer, etc), but they are a deeply ingrained part of us. This is what led me to decide to write this series.

By recognizing these 34 talents, and how they show up for you, you will build confidence naturally. For me, a lack of confidence is merely a symptom of a lack of self-awareness. I want you to see yourself in a positive light and understand just how much your talents guide and lead you through your daily life - from relationships to how you spend your free time and everything in between.

My hope is that this book sheds light on something you may have taken for granted. That you now see your talent as something special, something to be valued, and something unique to *you*. Also, how you can now harness this talent to build a strength and how to recognize when and/or it might be getting in the way.

In strength and love

1L

How to Use This Book

Obviously, your first thought is to read about your own talents. However, I hope you share this book with others and use it to try and understand them better as well. This book is divided by domains versus alphabetical order. Here's what you'll find included for each talent:

Quick Reference (The "Twitter" statement)
This brief description summarizes the beauty of your talent. You can even find the "Quick Tip" sheet for each of them on this web page:
http://discoverjoself.com/resources

The Gallup® Definition
This is how Gallup® defines each talent and what anyone with this talent will recognize.

Celebrate & Evaluate
Here you'll find four bullet points under each heading.

Celebrate: I want you to see the amazing value your talent brings to the table. These are ways in which you shine.

Evaluate: You'll find questions to ask yourself to help you harness your talent and be aware of when it might be hindering you instead of helping you.

Descriptions are divided into two sections:

WHAT WILL HELP YOU

How to recognize it: This is considered to be useful for both personal reflection as well as helpful for others to better understand what the talent's communication style looks like.

How it might frustrate others: This highlights the characteristics of the talent's style which might irritate others. There is a general frustration as well as ones that are particular to the other domains.

Something to Consider: A word of advice on the communication traps the talent might easily fall into and how to avoid them.

WHAT WILL HELP OTHERS CONNECT WITH YOU

Questions to Connect: Questions that will open the communication channels in order to connect more easily with someone who has this talent. The questions can certainly be self-reflective as well.

Tips for Connection: Suggestions on how to enter a dialogue or make a better connection with someone who has this talent and an extra word of advice on how we might keep the talent away from its dark side.

Have fun. Explore. Talk about it with your friends and family. And, most of all, discover the power to connect within YOU.

Quick Reference: Communication Styles

You can find a downloadable copy of these "Twitter" statements at http://discoverjoself.com/resources

ACHIEVER®: Your communication style contributes energy, stamina, and intensity to any conversation. You seek to get things done, so getting to the point is essential for you.

ACTIVATOR®: Your communication style contributes a sense of urgency and equally contagious energy which easily motivates others to get moving and take action.

ADAPTABILITY®: Your communication style contributes flexibility of thought, an openness to follow the lead of change, and an ability to respond appropriately and thoughtfully in the moment.

ANALYTICAL®: Your communication style contributes a needed objectivity and level-headed approach, especially when emotions are running high.

ARRANGER®: Your communication style contributes flexible thinking which enhances your collaborative approach to effectively accomplish the goal at hand.

BELIEF®: Your communication style contributes clarity and conviction underscored with a defined set of values so others will always know where you stand.

COMMAND®: Your communication style contributes strength of conviction in times of calm and emotional clarity when tensions arise.

COMMUNICATION®: Your communication style brings attention to messages which need to be heard by finding just the right words to convey what needs to be said.

COMPETITION®: Your communication style contributes a contagious energy and enthusiasm which rallies others to do their best and rise to the top.

CONNECTEDNESS®: Your communication style contributes a full-picture perspective not only of how things connect but their effect on one another.

CONSISTENCY®: Your communication style contributes a transparent and fair set of expectations which promotes a culture of stability and predictability.

CONTEXT®: Your communication style contributes questions and insights that draw a thread through where we come from and aim it to where we are going.

DELIBERATIVE®: Your communication style contributes a careful consideration of thought and selection of words which, in turn, provide a thoughtful and conscientious approach to most matters.

DEVELOPER®: Your communication style contributes consistent recognition of progress being made and your delivery is notably tranquil and patient.

DISCIPLINE®: Your communication style is very direct and contributes precision of thought and clear details on what is expected.

EMPATHY®: Your communication style contributes comfort with expressing your emotions often putting others at ease to express theirs.

FOCUS®: Your communication style contributes an ability to boil down the complex, into a clear and targeted direction.

FUTURISTIC®: Your communication style contributes inspiration and vision, always exploring "What if?" and "What could be".

HARMONY®: Your communication style contributes tranquility and calmness to negotiate easily with all parties in order to establish a common ground.

IDEATION®: Your communication style contributes quick thinking, fresh perspectives, and a desire to share all ideas - good and bad - because you never know where the inspiration will be born.

INCLUDER®: Your communication style contributes a kind and collaborative tone, which lends itself to being a voice for others who may not be heard.

INDIVIDUALIZATION®: Your communication style contributes flexibility and creativity in the way you speak, meeting people where they are, and by speaking in a tone or manner they will understand.

INPUT®: Your communication style contributes an obvious wealth of information and resources that you are eager to share.

INTELLECTION®: Your communication style contributes a thoughtful approach, generating new, complex, and valuable thoughts that inspire others, frame a course of action or set strategic direction.

LEARNER®: Your communication style contributes a natural curiosity about people and subjects, which leads to thoughtful questions and an open mind to new ways of doing things.

MAXIMIZER®: Your communication style contributes high quality through your carefully selected words and expressions.

POSITIVITY®: Your communication style contributes obvious energy, enthusiasm, and an ability to encourage others in challenging circumstances.

RELATOR®: Your communication style contributes genuine and authentic connection through deep and empathetic conversation.

RESPONSIBILITY®: Your communication style contributes a high standard of commitment, integrity, and promises kept.

RESTORATIVE™: Your communication style contributes a constructively critical and courageous approach to problems in order to ensure the best solutions.

SELF-ASSURANCE®: Your communication style contributes confident and thoughtful opinions, formed from personal experience, which offers reassurance to others in tough situations.

SIGNIFICANCE®: Your communication style contributes purpose and impact as you inspire others with your vision for a successful and sustainable legacy.

STRATEGIC®: Your communication style contributes enthusiastic energy and creative imagination, offering several options to find the best path to the desired outcome.

WOO®: Your communication style contributes an enthusiasm to connect and know others through your warm and engaging manner.

1l

WHAT would HAPPEN if we studied what was *right* with people VERSUS what's *wrong* with people?

Don Clifton

Photo courtesy of Gallup, Inc. Used with permission.

EXECUTING

Look at a day when you are supremely satisfied at the end. It's not a day when you lounge around doing nothing; it's a day you've had everything to do and you've done it.

Margaret Thatcher

EXECUTING DOMAIN

According to Gallup: Team members who have a dominant strength in the Executing domain are those whom you turn to time and again to implement a solution. These are the people who will work tirelessly to get something done. People who are strong in the Executing domain have an ability to take an idea and transform it into reality within the organization they lead.

Talents in this Domain

**Achiever   Arranger   Belief
Consistency   Deliberative   Discipline
Focus   Responsibility   Restorative**

Do you know someone high in Executing talents? You know, those "Doers", the ones who love to get things done? Did you know they have a certain communication style?

Those who are high in Executing talents are "to the point" speakers. In general, they tend to speak in bullet points and appreciate specific answers. Too much chit-chat can get in the way of getting things done. They will welcome extra details - if they ask for them. So be prepared to offer a strong summary statement but have the details to back up your point - just in case.

Executing folks are generally pretty confident, so they won't take your short answers as anything other than respecting their time.

Typical Characteristics
- Self-motivated
- Duty-oriented and results-focused
- Cares about efficiency
- Knows how to make things happen
- Will work tirelessly to get it done
- Can "catch" an idea and make it a reality

Communication Style
- In general, likes to receive and give bullet-point-type communication
- Often gets to the point
- Needs specificity
- Conversation focuses on end results
- Doesn't want to chat. Prefers to speak and act quickly
- Prefers overviews, but with details ready, if needed
- Direct, decisive, and confident

Things They Might Say or Do
- What's expected of me?
- What's the deadline?
- What's the desired outcome?
- What's the goal?
- List out their plan of action e.g. "I think we need to do, 1, 2, 3…"
- Likely to be bored if a decision hasn't been made yet
- Start taking action before a final decision has been made
- Might hear ideas as something they need to do now

Michèle S. Switzerland

I manage diverse teams of senior leaders in a large global organisation. All teams have clear strategic goals, defined actions, and responsibilities. My Achiever not only keeps track of my own to-do list but also a list for each team I work with. I make sure they do what they committed to and remind them when they haven't. Luckily, my Individualization & Relator help me strike a balance between being too pushy and getting stuff done, but the Achiever always wants to move things forward.

When I am passionate about something, I don't easily take "no" for an answer, continuing to push other avenues that might get the same result. My teams of senior partners appreciate the fact that I keep them accountable as long as I don't push too hard. My work peers have voiced that they are "intimidated" by my efficiency - and slightly annoyed as I get a lot of stuff done. My manager needs to remind me to slow down and check-in on my work-life balance from time to time.

Unchecked, my Achiever might seem unfriendly, cold, and too driven. Especially in stressful situations, I must remind myself to take time to chitchat with people, write a short "how are you?" at the beginning of my emails, or just pick up the phone instead of writing a one-line e-mail requesting a status update."

Achiever®

Communication for ACHIEVER®

> *Your communication style contributes energy, stamina, and intensity to any conversation. You seek to get things done, so getting to the point is essential for you.*

According to Gallup®: People exceptionally talented in the Achiever theme work hard and possess a great deal of stamina. They take immense satisfaction in being busy and productive.

Celebrate:

- How goals drive you
- Your to-do lists
- Your ability to work hard
- How you get things done

Evaluate:

- Am I becoming a workaholic?
- Am I expecting the same intensity from others?
- Am I forgetting about self-care?
- Am I adding too many things to my list?

WHAT WILL HELP YOU

How to recognize it: You are ready to complete whatever task is at hand. This means you likely have a list of what needs to be done and follow it pretty closely. When speaking with others, you are brief, concise, and to the point. You also need clear expectations and will ask - perhaps to the point of pestering - until you have clarity on the ultimate goal. Your style is directive and will be especially noticed in emails, where you likely say exactly what needs to be said, foregoing formalities and icebreaking.

How it might frustrate others: Your intensity and focus may come across as being more important than the people in the conversation.
For Influencers: You may forget to share the 'why' behind what you're doing, preventing them from knowing exactly how they impact the overall mission
For Relationship Builders: You may forget to take a moment to connect personally. A simple "hello" and "how are you?" can go a long way in maintaining good relationships.
For Strategic Thinkers: You may take action before a plan has been fully determined.

Something to consider: Watch out for your natural work-to-get-it-done bias. Remember to consider the needs of others as well and what their task list might involve. You may find you are working toward the same goal if you take a beat and listen.

WHAT WILL HELP OTHERS CONNECT WITH YOU

Questions to Connect

- What's your/the goal?
- What did you achieve last year?
- What accomplishment are you most proud of?
- What do you need to do on this to feel complete?
- What's keeping you from moving forward?

Tips for Connection

- Be as concise and direct as possible.
- Start with the goal in mind and connect to what the Achiever has in mind as the end result.
- *Word of caution:* Since people high in Achiever can be counted on to get things done, be sure you're not adding to their list unwittingly. You may forget what you've asked them to do and unknowingly overload their list. Also, let them know what they *don't* need to do, otherwise, they may do it anyway.

My Arranger has perhaps more influence than I thought over my listening.

Arranger is about efficiency and organisation; this means when I listen or read, I am quick to infer meaning; make sense of things and fill in gaps. I'm a speed reader and I probably do this when listening too. That's good and bad – I can pick up on the unspoken (sometimes uncannily so) but I might also jump to the wrong conclusions; or finish other people's sentences (very bad, I know!). My family calls me impulsive, but I always feel this is a wrong diagnosis - I just think things through very quickly!!

When communicating to others in a prepared way, my organised brain writes and talks in a way that is logical and helps people understand the context and the call to action. There are usually no questions about something I have written or presented from a checking understanding point of view. I am clear! I am constantly checking for gaps in info and won't be afraid to repeat back what I have understood to check we are both on the same page, so I guess my Arranger is helping me structure a conversation in the moment too!

Arranger®

Communication for ARRANGER®

Your communication style contributes flexible thinking which enhances your collaborative approach to effectively accomplish the goal at hand.

According to Gallup®: People exceptionally talented in the Arranger theme can organize, but they also have a flexibility that complements this ability. They like to determine how all of the pieces and resources can be arranged for maximum productivity.

Celebrate:

- Your ability to multitask
- The drive to focus on multiple projects
- Your ability to simplify complex arrangements
- Your flexibility

Evaluate:

- Am I overscheduling myself or others?
- Do I lose focus by juggling too many balls at once?
- Do things fall through the cracks?
- Am I too controlling of others' schedules or routines?

WHAT WILL HELP YOU

How to recognize it: You frequently take on the role of coordinator when ideas are being shared. You love to explore possible outcomes by shuffling ideas, people, and tasks around to find the most successful approach to the plan. With your ability to see how the group can work together in a dynamic situation, you can communicate how work can get done by the 'we'. When a project is complete, you ruminate over the process and how to enhance it for the next time so you can leverage it going forward.

How it might frustrate others: Your tendency to continually re-arrange for optimal efficiency might confuse others who can't keep track of the changes.
For Influencers: If the purpose of your plans isn't clear, they may tune out and choose not to be a part of what you're creating.
For Relationship Builders: People keen to have strong relationships may feel left out or neglected if they aren't included in your plans.
For Strategic Thinkers: If you are constantly rearranging plans, those in this domain may have a hard time keeping up and wonder what the exact plan really is.

Something to Consider: You love to multitask, however, be wary of getting involved in more than you can effectively handle or of overscheduling - yourself and others. Evaluate just how much time, space, and energy you have to organize work teams, projects, your social life, and your family.

WHAT WILL HELP OTHERS CONNECT WITH YOU

Questions to Connect

- How would you prioritize the projects in front of us?
- What patterns do you see in these examples?
- How will you organize the teams?
- Imagining everything is organized how you like it, what does that look like?
- What do you need in order to plan effectively?

Tips for Connection

- Arrangers love to multi-task which may look like they aren't focused, but switching between projects or tasks is what keeps them going and full of energy.
- Arrangers need space and autonomy to arrange and rearrange, however, they also need a framework or boundaries within which to work and flex their skill.
- *Word of caution:* Before asking someone with Arranger to help on a project or a task, make sure they don't already have too many balls in the air and can handle taking on more or can decide which one to drop.

Nate W, USA

The Upside:

I am an advocate for anything I am passionate about—whether it is a restaurant, clothing line, or new exercise routine. I readily share the benefits of my passion with anyone who will listen. Being the messenger helps me influence others' decisions. For example, after being introduced to and understanding CliftonStrengths I shared it with everyone. My passion continues today, years later, as I coach people and teams.

The Downside:

As a parent of four children between the ages of 15 and 7, my Belief talent can get set off nearly every day. When my core beliefs/values are challenged, I very quickly and easily spiral into whatever sets them off. For example, bedtime is the worst time of the day for me. When I ask kids to get ready for bed, they push back or ignore me which triggers my "mutual respect" belief. On bad days, my kids' disrespect of me turns into my disrespecting them. We spiral downward until I am able to compose myself and realize what I've done.

Belief®

Communication for BELIEF®

> *Your communication style contributes clarity and conviction underscored with a defined set of values so others will always know where you stand.*

According to Gallup®: People exceptionally talented in the Belief theme have certain core values that are unchanging. Out of these values emerges a defined purpose for their lives.

Celebrate:

- Your deeply developed values
- Your sense of meaning and purpose
- Your altruistic nature
- Your strong sense of integrity

Evaluate:

- Am I too set in my ways?
- Am I open to others belief systems?
- Are my opinions too strong or too rigid?
- Am I not allowing for "grey areas"?

WHAT WILL HELP YOU

How to recognize it: People will always know how you feel about certain topics or issues. Combined with your strong values, you communicate with clarity, conviction, and passion, especially in areas where you hold strong beliefs or feelings. If a project or task is out of alignment with your beliefs, it will be difficult to motivate you to be a part. Your deeply held beliefs provide personal power to stand strong no matter what.

How it might frustrate others: If you stick too fiercely to your beliefs without respecting or listening to how others might feel, you could create rifts unintentionally. *For Influencers:* Because purpose and a clear 'why' are important to both, it's essential to be in alignment otherwise conflicts could arise.
For Relationship Builders: The biggest challenge will arise if there aren't shared values. In order to connect and trust, you need to be able to relate to one another.
For Strategic Thinkers: They may consider you to be closed off and closed-minded if you aren't able to discuss differing ideas with you in a thoughtful way.

Something to consider: You may come across as narrow-minded, stubborn, or inflexible. Even if you disagree with another's viewpoint, be respectful, listen carefully, and remember that most of us lead with positive intention.

WHAT WILL HELP OTHERS CONNECT WITH YOU

Questions to Connect

- What values do you believe are missing or lacking?
- What issues or topics are you most passionate about?
- What are some ideas that you value strongly?
- What do you believe about...?
- Which values most guide your decision-making?

Tips for Connection

- Listen carefully to which values are being referred to or insinuated when having a conversation. These clues can be invaluable to moving forward.

- Find which values you have in common. This will help establish trust.

- *Word of caution:* What may look like stubbornness, might just be steadfastness due to deep convictions. Ask questions and explore to get to the root of what might be happening if a conflict arises.

Cheryl P. Missouri, USA

I easily recognize how my Consistency influences my communication style. I'm process-oriented and efficient so when I speak with others I make my expectations and meaning clear. My strong sense of fairness means that I make sure what I say is clear to everyone. And I make sure that everyone has the opportunity to have input. I'm very good at proof-reading and can find inconsistencies in documentation that others might not see. I prefer written commitments over verbal to be sure that everyone is on the same page and all details are included. I may frustrate others because of the level of details I ask for and the repetitive nature of process planning. But in the end, I believe they appreciate the final process map or planning documents that are the result of our communication.

Consistency®

Communication for CONSISTENCY®

> *Your communication style contributes a transparent and fair set of expectations which promotes a culture of stability and predictability.*

According to Gallup®: People exceptionally talented in the Consistency theme are keenly aware of the need to treat people the same. They crave stable routines and clear rules and procedures that everyone can follow.

Celebrate:

- Your clear expectations
- Your fairness
- How you treat others equally
- Your ability to set clear boundaries

Evaluate:

- Am I more concerned with rules than people?
- Are rigid expectations prioritized over responding to the needs of others?
- Am I enforcing rather than discussing or understanding?
- Is my way the only way?

WHAT WILL HELP YOU

How to recognize it: As you naturally promote fairness, you are often the voice for rules, policies, and equality in your interactions. This leads you to speak with others in an efficient and clear manner, always ensuring expectations or guidelines are clear and the same for everyone. You are the one to point out inconsistencies in rules or mass communications that others may not spot. You might prefer things in writing over verbal commitments to be sure everyone is on the same page and details aren't left out.

How it might frustrate others: Your need for fairness and clear rules may come across as inflexible or possibly even inconsiderate to others.
For Influencers: Your need to keep things predictable could be interpreted as thinking small and being unable to take a needed risk.
For Relationship Builders: Your apparent preference for a one-size-fits-all approach, may feel as if individual preferences or needs don't matter.
For Strategic Thinkers: Your need for a clear process and guidelines may leave them feeling challenged to explore "what-if" scenarios with you.

Something to consider: You may come across as inflexible or too rigid to others, with rules seeming to be more important to you than people. In some instances, exceptions to rules or policies may need to be made. Make sure to listen to others and consider their position.

WHAT WILL HELP OTHERS CONNECT WITH YOU

Questions to Connect

- In your opinion, is this fair?
- How will this be perceived by the people involved?
- Do you feel balanced?
- Where do you see inconsistencies?
- Who's not being treated fairly in this situation?

Tips for Connection

- Consider emailing them when drawing up rules, policies, or procedures. They will appreciate the clarity and time to review them first.

- They are keenly tuned into any sense of favoritism or different rules for different people. They are a great touchpoint to consider when delegating roles or tasks to keep balance among the team or in the family.

- *Word of caution:* Keep situations as predictable as possible. Surprises or a break in protocol might throw them off balance.

Holly M. California, USA

Meetings without agendas make me crazy! My Deliberative needs to anticipate what will be discussed so I can be prepared with answers. I've gone so far as to decline meetings that didn't include an agenda or a descriptive subject line. (Unless, of course, they were from my boss!)

I can't tell you how many conversations I've rehearsed in my head, with different variations, before they ever happen. One memorable situation happened in the Dallas Fort Worth airport. I needed to check in with the gate agent. I anticipated she would ask, "How may I help you?" I had rehearsed my response and was ready for her question. However, when I reached the counter, she didn't say anything, so I spoke first and said, "How may I help you?" Yes, I got a very strange look, but after an awkward moment she took care of my situation.

Deliberative®

Communication for DELIBERATIVE®

Your communication style contributes a careful consideration of thought and selection of words which, in turn, provide a thoughtful and conscientious approach to most matters.

According to Gallup®: People exceptionally talented in the Deliberative theme are best described by the serious care they take in making decisions or choices. They anticipate obstacles.

Celebrate:

- Your vigilance
- Your perspective from multiple points of view
- Your conscientiousness
- You measure risk carefully and move forward accordingly

Evaluate:

- Am I too afraid of making the wrong decision?
- Am I playing Devil's Advocate just to be contrary?
- Am I holding others back with my cautiousness?
- Am I unwilling to trust decisions from others?

WHAT WILL HELP YOU

How to recognize it: You give voice to the potential risks in a given path, as well as ways to mitigate that risk. You are thoughtful about what you want to say and how you want to say it. You are efficient in your delivery of what needs to be communicated. It's possible you may have a minority viewpoint, but it may be just the viewpoint that the group needs to have the greatest possibility for success.

How it might frustrate others: Your reserved and quiet nature may inadvertently have others perceive you as difficult to approach, aloof, uninterested, or unfriendly.

For Influencers: Your perceived obstacles may interfere with their vision and they may even see it as pessimism.

For Relationship Builders: Your quietness may be interpreted as lacking the desire to connect.

For Strategic Thinkers: Your constant observation of obstacles may be viewed as impeding their ability to plan and create a vision.

Something to consider: Due to your tendency to overthink in a vacuum without taking action - or sharing with others - you may be seen as not contributing to the dialogue or be disengaged. Let people know that you are carefully considering what is being said and will contribute your thoughts—perhaps toward the end of the meeting or in a follow-up e-mail.

WHAT WILL HELP OTHERS CONNECT WITH YOU

Questions to Connect

- What are the potential risks given the current situation?

- What red flags do you see?

- What needs to be considered before taking action?

- How much time do you need to think about this?

- What information are you missing?

Tips for Connection

- Be prepared to get them to expand on their thinking as they may not fully communicate all the thoughts in their head.

- When asking them for a decision, be sure to give them time to consider their response, even if it's just about where to go for dinner.

- *Word of caution:* Because they have a terrible fear of being wrong - or saying the wrong thing - they may overly delay speaking up. Ask them how much time they need to make a well-informed choice, but be prepared to negotiate the amount of time they really have.

Kellie F. Massachusetts, USA

While listening to a "Theme Thursday" podcast, I heard the phrase "referee for relevance." It describes my communication style perfectly. I want to know and share with others the important information and what the plan is. My motivation is to ensure they have as few questions as possible. I communicate so that everyone is on the same page, knows expectations, and can move forward on equal footing.

The downside is I can easily get annoyed when people don't remember or access the communication I provided. I am guilty of thinking things such as "I told you this already," "Did you even read my email?" and other not-so-positive thought bubbles.

Recently a new colleague high in Context shared that while my documentation of topics was impeccable, it didn't provide them with enough framework to understand fully. This was a great learning moment and reminder that even as a Strengths-Coach, I need to remember the strengths of others!

Discipline®

Communication for DISCIPLINE®

Your communication style is very direct and contributes precision of thought and clear details on what is expected.

According to Gallup®: People exceptionally talented in the Discipline theme enjoy routine and structure. Their world is best described by the order they create.

Celebrate:

- How you easily break down big tasks
- Your ease with efficiency
- Your attention to detail
- Your ability to maintain a routine or schedule

Evaluate:

- Am I too rigid with others?
- Am I willing to be flexible when necessary?
- Am I too hard on others with their inattention to detail?
- Am I unwilling to change?

WHAT WILL HELP YOU

How to recognize it: You create very ordered, precise communications that help generate clarity. You tend to think - and speak - in bullet points. Short, sweet, and to the point is your motto. You tackle most tasks with structure and efficiency, creating a step-by-step process that keeps you at the top of your game - and it's what you expect from others as well.

How it might frustrate others: Your need for order can dampen the beauty of the natural "chaos" of more flexible family, friends, and co-workers.
For Influencers: Your rigidity to the routine may rub them the wrong way as they love to dream big and need the flexibility to achieve what they desire.
For Relationship Builders: Your need for structure and routine may be seen as cold and inflexible and not considerate of the type of structure others might need.
For Strategic Thinkers: Your routines or contentment with the status quo may keep them from fully exploring possibilities in their own plans and processes.

Something to consider: Chaos and confusion are likely totally frustrating to you, and when people are flying by the seat of their pants, you likely feel stressed. The inherent messiness of humans is a given and since your need for order is greater than most, be prepared to flex in some aspects - even a small compromise can garner big gains.

WHAT WILL HELP OTHERS CONNECT WITH YOU

Questions to Connect

- Would you like to set up the schedule?
- How do you think we could better organize our time here?
- What routines/habits do you need to implement?
- How can we be more efficient?
- Help me understand your system.

Tips for Connection

- Ask them about what they need to feel prepared and what routines are important to them and their well-being or ability to tackle a task.
- Be prepared for brief encounters that are task-focused. It's not personal, it's for efficiency on their part.
- *Word of caution:* If change is imminent, make sure to give them a heads-up, possibly before others need to know, so they can prepare themselves both mentally, emotionally, and physically.

Kristin D. Ed.D. California, USA

In the past when working in groups, I often was the person to keep the group moving forward and following up on what action items we needed to meet deadlines. As a meeting finished, I was often the person to take the variety of ideas and conversations and focus the team on the most important tasks that had to get done. I always thought this was due to my Achiever and Responsibility, yet as I have had the opportunity to spend more time learning about my 6-10 strengths, I have come to realize my Focus is what helps me prioritize, and get a team to meet the expectations or goals set before us. As an Achiever, I always have a running list, but my Focus pushes me to prioritize which of the items on that list I need to get done first so I can stay on track. Recently, my team hosted a week-long program with 15 different workshops. We had many loose ends to tie up the project and get a final email out to the participants. Due to unforeseen circumstances, no one had determined who would do the wrap-up items. I utilized my Focus to identify what needed to get done, check in with teammates to delegate tasks, and confirm the completion of each item to efficiently wrap up by sharing resources and news with attendees. It was my ability to target what was needed and reprioritize my workday that put a successful bow on the event.

Focus®

Communication for FOCUS®

> *Your communication style contributes an ability to boil down the complex, into a clear and targeted direction.*

According to Gallup®: People exceptionally talented in the Discipline theme enjoy routine and structure. Their world is best described by the order they create.

Celebrate:

- Your ability to prioritize tasks
- Your targeted drive
- Your ability to zero-in on important details
- Your concentration superpower

Evaluate:

- Am I too focused on the details to see the big picture?
- Am I placing my priorities over the needs of others?
- Am I listening closely enough to others who might not have the same goals?
- Are my goals more important than people?

WHAT WILL HELP YOU

How to recognize it: When others are taking a conversation in many different directions, you can clearly and concisely boil it down to simple and clear objectives. This helps focus the group on the most important tasks to be done or ideas to be developed. You need to have clear priorities, so it's important for you to be able to come to an agreement on what exactly needs to be done and by when. You are direct and to the point, as your time and energy are precious to you.

How it might frustrate others: Your laser-targeted viewpoint may appear to be a bit short-sighted to others.

For Influencers: There may be a struggle to match priorities and how the short-term goals impact the overall desire.

For Relationship Builders: Your need for time and space to concentrate may appear as being aloof and distant.

For Strategic Thinkers: If your priorities aren't in alignment with what needs to be solved first, planning could be a challenge.

Something to Consider: You likely are easily frustrated when priorities keep shifting or people go off on tangents. Remember, not all solutions come from linear thinking and something off the beaten path could lead to something better. Work on your flexibility to keep relationships balanced.

52

WHAT WILL HELP OTHERS CONNECT WITH YOU

Questions to Connect

- What time of day are you most productive?
- What's the target? Is that the right target?
- How would you prioritize this?
- What causes you to lose focus?
- What's your biggest priority right now?

Tips to Connect

- Ask how much time and space they need to accomplish what they are working on and then work with them to find a balance.
- Come to an agreement on priorities and don't assume you see them the same as they do.
- *Word of caution:* People with Focus require uninterrupted space. Allow them to find a quiet place to concentrate and don't take it personally if they break away from the pack for a bit.

Angeline S. Missouri, USA

My role as a project manager is to ensure client commitments are met, which is made possible when project team members, myself included, keep our commitments. A glimpse into our team communication sounds like this: "Can you please complete the technical requirements by Monday so I can update the project schedule? Schedule updates are due to the client every Tuesday. Please confirm you received this, and that the Monday deadline is doable."

For me, delivering the schedule to clients on time means I am keeping my commitment. But since I depend on others for the schedule, I also have a need for my teammates to reciprocate their responsibilities, and I get that by explicitly asking for their confirmation.

Another relevant example: Upon receiving Jo's email on writing about how my Responsibility communicates, I promptly responded with, "Jo, I will be sending my write-up to you this weekend", and because I sent it, I know I will see this request through.

Responsibility®

Communication for RESPONSIBILITY®

Your communication style contributes a high standard of commitment, integrity, and promises kept.

According to Gallup®: People exceptionally talented in the Responsibility theme take psychological ownership of what they say they will do. They are committed to stable values such as honesty and loyalty.

Celebrate:

- Your word is your bond
- People trust you
- Honoring your commitments
- Your accountability

Evaluate:

- Am I micromanaging?
- Do I have clear boundaries?
- Am I over-committed?
- When do I say no?

WHAT WILL HELP YOU

How to recognize it: People count on you because when you say you will do something, you do it. You inspire others, setting an example with your integrity and commitment. You give - and expect - clarity around roles, duties, and end results. You help people see why their responsibilities matter and what is at stake. You may have a tendency to speak more about the "me" than the "we" - meaning you take personal accountability for what needs to be done. You value your commitment, and you expect others to uphold their end of the promise as well.

How it might frustrate others: Your need to ensure that things get done can easily fall into micromanagement or nagging of others and the feeling you don't trust them.

For Influencers: Your need to keep a promise to someone may rub them the wrong way if they perceive the same outcome can be achieved through influencing other people.

For Relationship Builders: Your "do-it-myself" approach may not be appreciated as they prefer to work as a team.

For Strategic Thinkers: Your need to focus on duties and roles for present goals, may have them feeling suffocated when trying to plan for the future.

Something to consider: Because you are so concerned about getting things done, you might have difficulty delegating work to others or micromanaging them when you do. Learn to empower others to participate in the work which will ultimately help them grow and learn.

WHAT WILL HELP OTHERS CONNECT WITH YOU

Questions to Connect

- Which of your commitments most bring life to you?
- Which of your commitments most drain you?
- What is your role in your current projects?
- How do you prevent taking on too much?
- When and how do you say 'no'?

Tips to Connect

- If you promise something to someone high in this talent, be sure to follow through. You will earn their trust more easily this way.

- Make sure they know their exact roles and duties so they aren't taking on the commitments of others to ensure success or completion.

- *Word of caution:* Be sure to check in and ask about what they are currently working on *and* how emotionally tied they feel to their current projects or roles. They may have said yes and are doing it just because they said they would - or because no one else would do it.

Leanna I. California, USA

My inclination with everything is to find a solution; if you communicate a problem, I cannot help but communicate a solution. There have been many instances in my career where I've offered solutions to my clients and co-workers and, exasperated, they tell me that all they truly needed was a chance to vent! Now, I try to get better at listening and creating a space for my clients and coworkers to unload. Additionally, my clients and coworkers are also getting better at prefacing conversations with "I just need to vent."

Restorative™

Communication for RESTORATIVE™

Your communication style contributes a constructively critical and courageous approach to problems in order to ensure the best solutions.

According to Gallup®: People exceptionally talented in the Restorative theme are adept at dealing with problems. They are good at figuring out what is wrong and resolving it.

Celebrate:

- How you solve problems
- The ease with which you handle difficult decisions
- Your commitment to doing things right
- Being solution-oriented

Evaluate:

- Is my focus more negative than positive?
- Am I fixated on problems rather than solutions?
- Am I being overly critical (of myself or others)?
- Is my viewpoint too narrow?

WHAT WILL HELP YOU

How to recognize it: You are someone who is perceived to see only what is broken. It's rarely personal. For you, calling out the problem is just seeing it for what it is. You then look for ways to solve it, desiring to leave it better than before. You are direct with your observations. You scrutinize most details ensuring that all possible issues are seen and dealt with accordingly.

How it might frustrate others: Your directness and comfort with identifying and expressing problems or failures may be viewed as being finicky or negative.
For Influencers: Your observations may be taken as criticisms and it could be difficult for them not to take it personally.
For Relationship Builders: You may automatically want to fix their problems when really, they likely just need to vent.
For Strategic Thinkers: Your perceptions of what's not working may be viewed as trying to poke holes in their ideas, even though they are still in the planning mode.

Something to consider: Be aware that your emphasis on problems is often seen as an inability to find anything positive and can feel like a personal attack if you're not careful. Learn to pivot from the problems you want to bring to others' attention and quickly create and apply practical solutions with swift action.

WHAT WILL HELP OTHERS CONNECT WITH YOU

Questions to Connect

- How can we improve this situation?
- What's it going to take to fix your current problems?
- Where are the cracks?
- How do we get back to the original greatness?
- What will make this really strong?

Tips to Connect

- When you have an idea or project, use them to help you poke holes in it so you can build it back stronger together.
- If faced with a challenge, they are a great person to connect with to diagnose what might be going wrong and then find ways for it to be solved
- *Word of caution:* Keep in mind that what you perceive as a negativity bias, is just their way of seeing the world. They are truly interested in leaving things better than they found them by fixing what they perceive as broken. You may just need to pull them into the solution space proactively.

INFLUENCING

The real beginning of influence comes
as others sense you are being influenced
by them — when they feel understood
by you — that you have listened deeply
and sincerely, and that you are open.

Stephen R. Covey

Influencing Domain

According to Gallup: People who are innately good at influencing are always selling the team's ideas inside and outside the organization. When you need someone to take charge, speak up, and make sure your group is heard, look to someone with the strength to influence.

Talents in this Domain

**Activator   Command   Communication
Competition   Maximizer
Self-Assurance   Significance   Woo**

Do you know someone high in Influencing talents? You know, the Motivators & the Sellers? The ones who love to pump others up and spread the word? Did you know they have a certain communication style?

Those who are high in Influencing talents want to be heard - and ensure that others are heard too. In general, they love to explore possibilities and "big picture" thinking. They want to be creative and love hearing new ideas - as well as expanding on them. On the downside, they can dominate the conversation and forget to listen. They also have a tendency to sound like they know what they're talking about, even when they're winging it.

Believe it or not, even if they sound right, they are quite open to others' opinions and thoughts, so don't let them overpower you. I should know, this is my dominant talent area!

Typical Characteristics

- Energetic
- Persuasive
- Creative
- Helps reach a broader audience
- Sells the ideas
- Speaks up and makes sure the team is heard
- Creates energy and expansion
- Stimulating and inspirational

Communication Style

- In general, prefers "big picture" conversations
- Likes time to discuss and explore possibilities
- Can do most of the talking
- Doesn't want to get bogged down in the details
- Open to new ideas
- Needs to feel heard

Things They Might Say or Do

- What's the big picture?
- What's the impact we're trying to make?
- Why are we doing this?
- What's the point?
- What are you/we trying to do here?
- Likely *not* to have a good poker face
- Likes to be a part of the planning process to understand the WHY
- Will question the overall vision if not in agreement
- Might appear argumentative when just looking for clarity

Janice H. Ohio, USA

While planning a Christmas DoTERRA Essential Oils event, I involved a person in my upline and a builder of mine. Options were given and they were both quick to respond to what type of booth they wanted to run, the food they would bring, and the items they would donate. The event went smoothly and everyone involved enjoyed themselves.

I do not try to dictate with this strength, but make people feel involved. It is a skill of getting things done in a timely manner. We are not going to talk about it for hours. This is what we plan to get done and we do it together.

I have been in countless meetings where there is constant talk and no action. This becomes very frustrating for someone who has Activator in their top five strengths. It happens to be my #1!

Activator®

66

Communication for ACTIVATOR®

> *Your communication style contributes a sense of urgency and equally contagious energy which easily motivates others to get moving and take action.*

According to Gallup®: People exceptionally talented in the Activator theme can make things happen by turning thoughts into action. They want to do things now, rather than simply talk about them.

Celebrate:

- Jumping in with no fear
- Your hands-on learning approach.
- Your ability to innovate.
- Asking "why not?" instead of "why?"

Evaluate:

- Am I rushing my decision?
- Do I act impulsively?
- Am I communicating my ideas clearly?
- Is my impatience warranted?

WHAT WILL HELP YOU

How to recognize it: One of your favorite questions is quite possibly, "Why not?" You enjoy disrupting the status quo and getting others on board with your innovative approaches to problem-solving. When others come to you with a problem, you may be quick to try and solve it without first waiting to hear if it's already been solved. Listen first, they might just be keeping you in the loop. You enjoy hands-on learning over theoretical study, knowing that making mistakes is part of your process.

How it might frustrate others: It's possible you interrupt others when you can see where a conversation is going or you speak quickly because you are anxious to share your ideas and others are taking too long to "get there".

For Executors: Your ability (and desire) to learn in the process may leave those who require more clarity and set expectations to feel rushed to make a decision without full buy-in.

For Relationship Builders: Your desire for action over conversation can have them feeling left out, unheard, and not brought on board.

For Strategic Thinkers: Your energy and passion might feel overwhelming and too improvised for those who prefer more time to process and plan their next move.

Something to consider: Ensure you aren't disrupting just for the sake of it. Connect with others who can be the soundboard to your unique ideas and get to the core of your energy-filled mindset. This space will help you find breakthrough moments to move projects forward and take action even when the status quo feels impenetrable.

WHAT WILL HELP OTHERS CONNECT WITH YOU

Questions to Connect

- What do you need to consider before taking action?
- What is the first step to getting started?
- What are the next right steps?
- Where do you see yourself taking action here?
- What do you need me to do right now?

Tips for Connection

- Start with the end result and then fill in the details. This will help an Activator understand that no action is needed and they can just listen.
- Give them opportunities to learn hands-on and at the moment. They learn best from their mistakes and personal experience while also having a high-risk tolerance. "Fail fast and fail forward" is their motto.
- *Word of caution:* Activators may appear to be procrastinators, but they really just need short deadlines. The pressure to act helps them focus, so be sure to have clear, short-term deadlines when giving them a project or task to complete.

Jo S. Mexico/USA

There are three vivid memories where I easily recognize my Command. First, my father traveled for work, so I took care of myself starting at age 16. When he returned home on Fridays, I would tell him my plans for the weekend. His response? "Would you care to phrase that as a question?" I would retort, "Why? You're my dad, if you have a problem with it, just tell me." It never occurred to me that I needed to ask him permission since as the authority figure he could just say 'no'.

Second, teachers and students frequently approached me to speak up for or on behalf of some person or some cause because "of all the people I know, I know *you* won't be afraid to say what needs to be said." Imagine this, at just 16 yrs old.

And finally, my favorite compliment ever from a friend was when he called me 'raw'. He meant that if you asked me a question, you needed to be prepared for the answer because I wouldn't sugarcoat or lie just to tell you what you wanted to hear. You could count on me for the truth – and he valued that.

Command®

Communication for COMMAND®

> *Your communication style contributes strength of conviction in times of calm and emotional clarity when tensions arise.*

According to Gallup®: People exceptionally talented in the Command theme have presence. They can take control of a situation and make decisions.

Celebrate:

- Your ability to take charge when needed
- How you keep cool in a crisis
- Your honest and candid nature
- Your willingness to confront tough situations

Evaluate:

- Am I being perceived as argumentative or forceful by others?
- Am I asking or am I telling?
- Do I take over even when not asked or I don't need to?
- Am I coming across as intimidating to others?

WHAT WILL HELP YOU

How to recognize it: When you speak, people listen. You literally command attention when you have something to say. You get straight to the point and don't mince words. When others shy away, you step up to the challenge. You also welcome conflict and those who challenge you as you see that as a path to resolution. Though you may not seem open to the ideas of others, you actually welcome differing opinions as that will bring the best solution or agreement. You can inspire others to courageously deal with their issues in the face of threats.

How it might frustrate others: Your assuredness in your approach may also make you appear inflexible or even inconsiderate of others' ideas.
For Executors: If you have a "my way or the highway" attitude, you could cause riffs in productivity and how things are done.
For Relationship Builders: Your intensity and directness may feel intimidating, thereby you may be a challenge to connect with and get to know.
For Strategic Thinkers: Because you challenge ideas, they may see you as inflexible and tough to find middle ground when in the planning process.

Something to consider: Your desire to tackle conflict head-on and ability to speak frankly is often intimidating to others. Remember to open space to others for asking questions or disagreeing as it may not seem apparent that you are welcome to opposing ideas.

WHAT WILL HELP OTHERS CONNECT WITH YOU

Questions to Connect

- When was the last time you rose up to the occasion during a crisis?
- What route should we take?
- What needs to happen now?
- Who should do what?
- What resources do you need?

Tips for Connection

- Listen to what they have to say but don't be afraid to offer a different viewpoint or challenge their ideas. They will actually appreciate this as they learn and grow through opposing viewpoints.

- If you have your own thoughts on a subject, share them. They highly appreciate people with a strong mind of their own.

- *Word of caution:* Those high in Command need strong leaders. They will respond best to those who are not "yes" people and will only respect those who they feel have high integrity and are willing to stand up for what's right.

Communication is my number one talent theme and I have a natural ease with and love of words. I can get a conversation going on almost any topic and keep it flowing. I create stories and content that engage people and help them connect emotionally to what is being said, enabling them to verbalise their thoughts out loud in an inclusive, non-judgmental space.

Once the conversation is flowing however, I want to keep it that way and as I love to multi-task, have unwittingly carried on conversing while walking away from my audience – down the passage, out the door – wherever my next task takes me! This naturally frustrates people (mostly my family) who cannot understand why I am unable to sit still and participate in genuine two-way communication, especially seeing as I love being part of any discussion and hearing others' opinions.

Communication®

Communication for COMMUNICATION®

Your communication style brings attention to messages which need to be heard by finding just the right words to convey what needs to be said.

According to Gallup®: People exceptionally talented in the Communication theme generally find it easy to put their thoughts into words. They are good conversationalists and presenters.

Celebrate:

- Your ability to tell a captivating story
- Your clear explanations
- Being a good sounding board for others
- Your verbal processing skills

Evaluate:

- Am I listening as much as I'm talking?
- Am I missing what others are saying because I'm planning what to say next?
- Am I being clear and concise?
- Am I repeating myself too much?

WHAT WILL HELP YOU

How to recognize it: You are careful with the words you choose because it is deeply important for you to be heard and understood. You are a natural editor and poor communications that don't effectively get the message across do not sit well with you. You are most comfortable with verbal expression; however, you may also enjoy writing in order to convey what you have to say.

How it might frustrate others: Your need to verbally process could lead others to think you need help solving a problem vs just needing a space or sounding board to dump your ideas out.

For Executors: Your need to think out loud may leave them wondering when - and on what - they can start taking action.

For Relationship Builders: They will love hearing your stories but will need time to share their stories with you as well. Keep in mind the old adage, "two ears, one mouth".

For Strategic Thinkers: They need time to process what you say and think things through before responding. Allow time for the "silences" and not jump in just to fill the "void".

Something to Consider: Ensure that you are regulating the amount of time you speak and the amount of time you listen. When especially passionate about something, you may dominate a conversation or interrupt so as not to forget your point.

WHAT WILL HELP OTHERS CONNECT WITH YOU

Questions to Connect

- Tell me the story of what you see going on here.
- Could you summarize this group discussion in a sentence or two?
- What illustration could help us understand this concept?
- With whom do you need to talk about this?
- Who is your best sounding board?

Tips for Connection

- Give feedback (physical or verbal) as you listen to what someone with Communication is saying. If they get the sense that you don't understand or aren't paying attention, they have a tendency to repeat themselves until they know you do.

- Be a great sounding board. If they want to run an idea by you, ask if they need help or just want to talk it through, that way, you both know what to expect from the conversation.

- *Word of caution:* Don't assume someone with this talent can always communicate effectively. They may prefer writing over speaking or they may prefer one-on-one conversations over presenting to large groups.

Jonathan M. Massachusetts, USA

As a highly competitive person, I am sensitive to competitive language and strive to avoid its use in my communications, especially with other competitive people. My professional communications are oriented towards sharing ideas, facilitating teamwork, and working towards common goals. I feel great when I win but tend to disengage when I lose or feel I won't be the best; even if I win, the other competitive people I work with may resent it and be more difficult to work with in the future. So, I direct my drive to compete inward; I am competing against my past self to improve, to do better than before.

Competition works well in situations where victory is definable and can be shared with everyone you're working with, so I limit calls to competition to short-term goals and projects. Much of my work measures progress through a continuous marginal improvement and competitive language may be discouraging if you feel like you can't win outright. I work with several groups that don't all have the same priorities, and competition can twist into defiance if we don't feel we're working together.

Competition®

Communication for COMPETITION®

Your communication style contributes a contagious energy and enthusiasm which rallies others to do their best and rise to the top.

According to Gallup®: People exceptionally talented in the Competition theme measure their progress against the performance of others. They strive to win first place and revel in contests.

Celebrate:

- How you embody the spirit of winning
- Winning together is as important as winning alone
- Your drive and tenacity that inspires
- Knowing where to set the bar

Evaluate:

- Am I being a sore loser?
- Is MY win becoming more important than OUR win?
- Am I setting the bar too high?
- Am I praising the effort, even if the outcome isn't as hoped?

WHAT WILL HELP YOU

How to recognize it: What can I do to improve? How can we do better? What will it take to beat the competition? These are questions you frequently utter - either to yourself or to others. You love encouraging others to do their best and challenging them to reach even farther than they might imagine possible. By reflecting on past wins, you find the path to inspire others to lead the group toward ambitious wins together.

How it might frustrate others: Your need to win, either personally or as a team, may come across as demanding and possibly be considered unattainable.
For Executors: You may set seemingly unattainable goals which will fluster them as they need some assurance of having success in their goals.
For Relationship Builders: If your standards don't take into consideration their abilities and situation, they might feel inadequate or unheard.
For Strategic Thinkers: Your style may come across as more challenging or trying to one-up someone instead of being open to exploring ideas and possibilities.

Something to consider: When encouraging others, make sure you are motivating them to reach their gold standard and not yours. Your bar may not be their bar - yet. And remember the group win always has more impact than the solo win. Channel individual victories to motivate your team and lead by example for coworkers, family, and others in your circles.

WHAT WILL HELP OTHERS CONNECT WITH YOU

Questions to Connect

- How do you know you are ahead?
- Are you ready to be the company/ department/division to be the first to achieve this?
- How would it feel to achieve this before anyone else?
- To what standard will you hold yourself?
- How will you measure success?

Tips for Connection

- Get aligned on how progress will be measured and what is the most important area for improvement. They will appreciate giving their input on this and being heard.

- Push them to go a bit further than even they think they can go. A challenge is motivating for them.

- *Word of caution:* Be careful not to casually compare them to someone else without having a good reason for doing so and the information to back up your observation. However, using someone else as a measure or standard to which they can attain can absolutely motivate them to push harder.

David Z. Washington DC, USA

Maximizer is a great talent to leverage while preparing and delivering a communication event. The drive to get the most out of the communication event prompts me to think about the audience, the medium, the time frame, and desired outcomes while preparing. A rushed Maximizer approach might be to cram as much content in as possible, but that would actually go against pedagogical research that reveals that "less is more" in teaching and learning. Consequently, my Maximizer pushes me to keep refining and editing my content so that the message and format I'm preparing are focused and make an impact.

At the point of delivery, Maximizer helps me make "on the spot" adjustments because I've gone through the work of clarifying and prioritizing my objectives. Cutting a piece of content or including something I previously edited are both options I use while maximizing the communication event.

Maximizer®

Communication for MAXIMIZER®

> *Your communication style contributes high quality through your carefully selected words and expressions.*

According to Gallup®: People exceptionally talented in the Maximizer theme focus on strengths as a way to stimulate personal and group excellence. They seek to transform something strong into something superb.

Celebrate:

- Your dedication to excellence
- Preferring quality over quantity
- Your focus on strengths
- Your motivational manner

Evaluate:

- Am I being a perfectionist?
- Is the outcome realistic?
- Are my expectations too high?
- Am I mirroring excellence or only demanding it?

WHAT WILL HELP YOU

How to recognize it: When you speak, you are conscious of the words you choose to communicate exactly what you mean. You likely prefer to be concise over verbose, knowing quality is more important than quantity. You also recognize that it's not always *what* you say but *how* you say it which will increase the effectiveness of your message.

How it might frustrate others: Your need to constantly improve may come across as being overly picky or difficult to please.

For Executors: Your seemingly never-ending need to improve things might have others feeling like they're on a hamster wheel and never really getting anything done.

For Relationship Builders: Your encouragement for them to be their best, their happiest, their brightest, etc may have them feeling that they aren't good enough and will disappoint you.

For Strategic Thinkers: Your need to focus on only the highest ROI elements and their need to explore all the possibilities might clash if not aimed at the same purpose.

Something to Consider: Be aware that your ability to see how and what to improve may come across as setting high expectations for those around you and creating unintentional pressure for them to live up to your vision. Share the vision, but then let them decide when they are ready.

WHAT WILL HELP OTHERS CONNECT WITH YOU

Questions to Connect

- What would take this from great to excellent?
- What potential do you see in this project?
- How can we improve this experience?
- How can you make this even better than what you've already done?
- What does the ideal outcome look like to you here?

Tips for Connection

- Be a mentor or help them find one. They love to surround themselves with successful people who can help them reach their own true potential.

- When giving feedback, always recognize what they do well first. Criticism is likely to fall on deaf ears unless you approach it from a "what could be better" angle. "You're doing ok, but you could be doing even better if you considered..." That approach will be most effective with them.

- *Word of caution:* Use caution when talking about weaknesses or what's not working. They prefer to focus on what's going right and how to make it even better. Too much negativity can decrease their motivation and engagement.

Anbern G. Illinois, USA

Years ago, a friend and I started a training company. We did teambuilding and leadership workshops. A mentor asked if we could provide team building for his clients. My reaction was, "Of course!" My friend, however, had a few concerns: The participants will be family businesses. We haven't had experience with this clientele, and she was hesitant. I appreciated that her concerns were valid, but I was confident we could do it. For me, it wasn't if we should. The question was, "How can we prepare ourselves for this undertaking?"

Self-Assurance grounds me in such a way that if I ride high with an ambitious goal, I don't float away and get lost. I am anchored in the thought that whatever happens, I can either succeed or learn.

Sometimes I sound confident, people think my opinions are set. But I want and need input. I'm not intimidated by people being good at what they do. I appreciate it when someone challenges my position on things so we can move together toward a shared goal.

Self-Assurance®

Communication for SELF-ASSURANCE®

Your communication style contributes confident and thoughtful opinions, formed from personal experience, which offers reassurance to others in tough situations.

According to Gallup®: People exceptionally talented in the Self-Assurance theme feel confident in their ability to take risks and manage their own lives. They have an inner compass that gives them certainty in their decisions.

Celebrate:

- Your internal confidence
- Your ability to provide reassurance when others are in doubt
- Your steadiness in rocky situations
- The confidence you instill in others

Evaluate:

- Am I being dismissive of the opinions of others?
- Am I being stubborn?
- Am I being too authoritative?
- Am I impatient with others' insecurities?

WHAT WILL HELP YOU

How to recognize it: You express your opinions freely and with conviction. This ease comes from having taken risks and testing your own boundaries - you know from which you speak. Your confidence is based in self-awareness, not simple arrogance. You speak from experience and observation. You encourage - and even inspire - people to speak their minds and stake their own ground.

How it might frustrate others: Your certainty and confidence may easily be perceived as arrogant or dismissive of others.
For Executors: Your high tolerance for risk may push others beyond their comfort zone and what they believe can actually be accomplished.
For Relationship Builders: Your experience or knowledge doesn't speak for them and they may feel you aren't considering their point of view.
For Strategic Thinkers: Your self-informed process for learning may leave out the thoughts and opinions of others who are eager to be a part of the process.

Something to consider: Be aware that your confidence of expression may seem like you have all the answers. Be sure to discover how others may complement your own point of view so you can inspire others to be as bold and loyal to their ideas.

WHAT WILL HELP OTHERS CONNECT WITH YOU

Questions to Connect

- What is your gut telling you?
- How can you make sure you're not railroading people?
- What does your experience tell you?
- What makes you so sure?
- How much risk are you willing to take?

Tips for Connection

- Give tasks or projects to them where they can be the decision maker and have full autonomy. They'll enjoy the chance to prove themselves.

- Ask them whose support they want. They want to be supported by other strong people who are willing to challenge them and push them.

- *Word of caution:* Just because what they say sounds like they know the answer, they likely are just confident about their own experience. Push back, and challenge them, but be careful to balance it with not doubting them or their awareness of what's at stake.

Abdulsatter A. Saudi Arabia

Even as a kid, I asked a lot of questions, not to further understand but to let everyone know I was there. Whether it was with family or friends or at school, the same incident happened to me in grade 6, my teacher once said, "You just can't stop asking." Now I understand why. It wasn't about learning, I just had to show up.

As an adult, I remember my boss once said to me, "You're the one who has to add value to every single meeting as you can't stay quiet!" Again it's that Significance in me where my drive is to show up and leave an impact.

With Significance I don't need permission to speak up, I know what to say and how to say it with confidence, leaving a great impact. I do understand my communication may get me into trouble when it's raw, but I have learned how to overcome this by experience - knowing when to speak up and when to keep quiet. One of my bosses taught me: be tough, be firm, and be precise - and this is how I steer my Significance now.

Significance®

Communication for SIGNIFICANCE®

> *Your communication style contributes purpose and impact as you inspire others with your vision for a successful and sustainable legacy.*

According to Gallup®: People exceptionally talented in the Significance theme want to make a big impact. They are independent and prioritize projects based on how much influence they will have on their organization or people around them.

Celebrate:

- Your free and independent spirit
- Your desire to make a positive difference
- Your drive to succeed
- Your comfort in the spotlight

Evaluate:

- Am I seeking recognition for the right things?
- Do I have a healthy balance between emotional and material success?
- Do I push others into the spotlight even if they are uncomfortable?
- Does my network serve a purpose or am I just "rubbing elbows"?

WHAT WILL HELP YOU

How to recognize it: You can easily become the "face" for whatever you believe in, be it topics, causes, or initiatives. You have a deep desire to have a meaningful impact through your words and contributions. You love to talk about the big picture and how to create a lasting impression; however, you are designed to lead by example and prefer to inspire by doing, as opposed to explaining, teaching, or talking.

How it might frustrate others: It's possible that your comfort in the spotlight could look like attention-hogging to others.

For Executors: Your need for credit and recognition may have a team feeling resentful when it was really a collective win.

For Relationship Builders: Your comfort being in the spotlight may overshadow and push others away, creating a void in the relationship.

For Strategic Thinkers: Your need for success may keep you - and others - from thinking big and taking more risks so as to ensure the desired outcome.

Something to consider: Be sure your messaging and vision have more of a 'we' approach than a 'me' one. Publicly recognize the contributions of others and you'll have an even more significant impact.

WHAT WILL HELP OTHERS CONNECT WITH YOU

Questions to Connect

- What do you feel your legacy will be?
- What is the impact of your actions in the projects you're a part of?
- Who are you helping right now?
- What can you do now to help more people?
- What would you be most inspired to "be the face" of?

Tips for Connection

- Ask what matters to them and then give them the opportunity to have the impact they so deeply desire.

- External validation is key to their self-esteem. Having a chance at a better title, certification, awards, or degrees will fulfill their need for credibility and respect.

- *Word of caution:* They always want to level up and exceed expectations. Know that when they are looking for confirmation of a job well done, it's not fishing for compliments, but rather a desire for acknowledgment of what they've achieved.

Jennifer M. N. Carolina, USA

I use my WOO strength (Winning Others Over) naturally by seeking the thrill of meeting new people and making connections to expand my network. I work in Emergency Management preparing for disasters. I used to see WOO as persuasion, but I found it was more about how I won over the respect and admiration of others due to how I interact with them rather than trying to convince them to approve of me or my ideas. I purposefully found out what people needed in their roles to be successful or better prepared and worked to meet their needs while aligning it with my job. I frequently visited staff during all shifts to discuss issues relating to their roles and either discussing options or coaching them in response and preparedness topics. I also enjoy meaningful discussions to draw people into conversations both in-person and online. Authentic conversation is the best way to connect with others as well as the best way for me to learn. It is because of this easy nature to converse and help others that I can Win Others Over.

WOO®

Communication for WOO®

Your communication style contributes an enthusiasm to connect and know others through your warm and engaging manner.

According to Gallup®: People exceptionally talented in the WOO theme love the challenge of meeting new people and winning them over. They derive satisfaction from breaking the ice and making a connection with someone.

Celebrate:

- Your ability to make everyone feel at home
- Your outgoing nature
- How you start conversations with ease
- You make socializing look easy

Evaluate:

- Am I coming off as shallow?
- Am I showing genuine interest in those I'm connecting with?
- Am I overshadowing others around me?
- Is my energy matching the room?

WHAT WILL HELP YOU

How to recognize it: You seek to connect with everyone in an engaging and meaningful way, even if only for a brief moment. You talk easily with others and make a great wingman for your friends and colleagues as you can help put them at ease in social situations. You are easily approachable and your social confidence is easily recognized - and often admired - by others.

How it might frustrate others: Your energy may not match the level of the room, causing others great discomfort or doubts about your sincerity.

For Executors: Your need to socially engage with everyone might appear to derail tasks and plans, keeping them from hitting their targets.

For Relationship Builders: Your ability to connect with anyone may feel insincere or frivolous and stymie their need for a real connection.

For Strategic Thinkers: Your conversive nature might feel overwhelming and unnecessary when a more thoughtful approach is needed.

Something to consider: Remember, you need to feel out others' reactions to your social prowess to make sure you're not coming off as superficial. Put genuine interest in every interaction to connect at a deeper level in old and new relationships alike.

WHAT WILL HELP OTHERS CONNECT WITH YOU

Questions to Connect

- Where might you meet new people?
- What's your favorite story about meeting new friends or co-workers?
- How would you persuade someone to join you in your projects?
- What group can you go to for energy?
- How do you harness WOO for *you*?

Tips for Connection

- Allow them to help you expand your network. As much as they enjoy building their own network, they love to be able to purposefully connect others as well.

- Talk with them, not just to them. They want to find shared interests and points in common. They will appreciate hearing your stories and you listening to theirs.

- *Word of caution:* Give them opportunities to be around other people. WOOs need to socialize, they are most energized by being around groups of people. They may not even need to interact, but just feeling the energy of the room can recharge their batteries.

RELATIONSHIP BUILDING

The meeting of two personalities is like the contact of two chemical substances: if there is any reaction, both are transformed.

Carl Gustav Jung

Relationship Building

According to Gallup: Relationship builders are the glue that holds a team together. Strengths associated with bringing people together -- whether it is by keeping distractions at bay or keeping the collective energy high -- transform a group of individuals into a team capable of carrying out complex projects and goals.

Talents in this Domain

**Adaptability   Connectedness   Developer
Empathy   Harmony   Includer
Individualization   Positivity   Relator**

Do you know someone high in Building Relationship talents? You know, the caring folks in your circle? The ones who always ask how you're doing and really want to know? Did you know they have a certain communication style?

Those who are high in Relationship talents love to tell stories and to hear yours as well. They are adept at building consensus and are generally empathetic and understanding. Expect to spend a little time on chit-chat - how they're doing, how you're doing, and really listening to them. This establishes trust and rapport, which is of great importance to the Relationship Builder. They're great listeners and are keen to hear what you have to say as well.

If someone high in this talent area asks how your day is, believe that they really want to know. They're not just being polite, they truly care.

Typical Characteristics

- People oriented and very loyal
- Understanding and empathetic
- Cooperative and flexible
- Glue that holds the team together
- Unique ability to help the group become much greater than the sum of its parts
- A team player and consensus builder

Communication Style

- Paragraphs and details
- Patient
- Good listener
- Transmits tranquility
- Encourages ideas and opinions
- Prefers to chat/connect before you start working
- In-person conversations vs email chains

Things They Might Say or Do

- How are you doing? (And they mean it)
- How are you feeling? (They really want to know)
- Asks very personalized questions or makes personalized comments
- Likely to be the host
- Be complimentary and considerate
- Always says please and thank you
- Prefers 1:1 conversations or smaller groups
- Likely to ask: Who is/needs to be involved?
- Often the first, if not only, to respond to emails

Anna P. Ontario, Canada

I used to believe that I was flaky as I found it so easy to chameleon into whomever I was with. Then I met Jo, she was amazing at teaching me about my Strengths. Now I know I am high (1st) Adaptability. WOW, my life makes sense! Life is fascinating when you can communicate with people with ease and grace.

I find I am quite capable of talking with people at their interest level. I can easily jump between business and casual with the flick of a thought. This actually grounds me and gives me the confidence to speak with anyone - one on one or in front of a crowd. Adaptability has become my favourite quality in me.

Adaptability also serves me very well as an Intuitive Reader. Being able to quickly understand the person in front of me allows our time together to be about them, finding solutions to their issues, strategically creating a path for their journey, and leaving them confident that they were heard and understood.

Knowing this is a true part of me has opened the world for me. My life is richer and fuller thanks to understanding Adaptability is a gift.

Adaptability®

Communication for ADAPTABILITY®

Your communication style contributes flexibility of thought, an openness to follow the lead of change, and an agility to respond appropriately and thoughtfully in the moment.

According to Gallup®: People exceptionally talented in the Adaptability theme prefer to go with the flow. They tend to be "now" people who take things as they come and discover the future one day at a time.

Celebrate:

- How you 'go with the flow'
- Your spontaneous nature
- How you adjust seamlessly to new situations
- Your flexibility

Evaluate:

- Is this change necessary?
- Am I blindly following others?
- Is my flexibility preventing clarity or understanding?
- Does this situation require a solid decision?

WHAT WILL HELP YOU

How to recognize it: You are quite adept at switching gears when the script or plan gets derailed. You are most concentrated on discussing what is happening here and now as opposed to how we got here or where we're going. You prefer to examine each situation as it presents itself and then decide the best approach.

How it might frustrate others: You may have a tendency to go with the flow and to not spend time adequately preparing. Sometimes 'winging it' isn't enough. Make sure to have a focus for your communication.

For Executors: Your fluid problem-solving approach may confuse or frustrate those who prefer to have plans and expectations more clearly drawn out.

For Influencers: Since you can easily change directions, they may feel you are non-committal and therefore challenging to keep on track for the big-picture goals.

For Strategic Thinkers: Your spontaneous nature might look like thoughtlessness or carelessness to those who prefer more detailed and thought-out plans.

Something to Consider: Remember, your hunger for variety should not come at the expense of the real goals. Take time to consider HOW and WHEN it's prudent to switch it up and when you need to prioritize ONE path.

WHAT WILL HELP OTHERS CONNECT WITH YOU

Questions to Connect

- Would you prefer a job where you do different things every day?
- How do you handle sudden changes?
- What are your contingency plans?
- Would you prefer to do 'x' or 'y'?
- What feels most important to you right now?

Tips for Connection

- Give them a bit of time and space to explore their thoughts before bringing them back into focus. The thoughtful wandering can bring them back to center faster.

- Prioritize them to aid in communications when a crisis arises or unexpected change happens.

- *Word of caution:* People with Adaptability can be overwhelmed by too many options or none at all. They appreciate having 2-3 options presented to them so they can choose the one they most prefer.

Valeyne G. Illinois, USA

I look at most events as intended or purposeful, not coincidental. Without even thinking about it, I naturally ask about and communicate the links I see between how things and people connect, as well as their effect on one another. For example, when I'm coaching someone and they share a situation with me, it is not uncommon for me to ask, "What might this situation be wanting to teach you?" or "What is the gift here?", recognizing that most events have a special meaning or purpose in our lives and it's for the better good of all of humanity. Other times, I may ask, "How is this connected to other events in your life?" to support others in seeing meaningful connections in their own lives.

I also have a strong intuitive sense that guides me and find myself saying, "I can't explain exactly why...but I just know it!". This can frustrate executing people if they don't see a grounded reason for why.

Connectedness®

Communication for CONNECTEDNESS®

> *Your communication style contributes a full-picture perspective not only of how things connect but their effect on one another.*

According to Gallup®: People exceptionally talented in the Connectedness theme have faith in the links among all things. They believe there are few coincidences and that almost every event has meaning.

Celebrate:

- How you trust your inner wisdom
- Your natural compassion for all living things
- Your ability to be a bridge-builder by bringing people together
- Your desire to be a part of something bigger

Evaluate:

- Am I coming off as naive?
- Am I waiting for circumstances to be "just right" before taking action?
- Are my personal boundaries blurry?
- Am I leaving too many things to fate instead of making a decision?

WHAT WILL HELP YOU

How to recognize it: Because you "tap into" a universal perspective, you seek to inspire collaborations and be a bridge builder in order to inspire innovation and progress which benefits everyone. You speak from the gut and trust what you have observed or felt. You readily share personal stories that relate to a person or situation - desiring to find ways to connect on a deeper level to others. You're more interested in drawing out what people have in common rather than what separates us.

How it might frustrate others: Because of your altruistic nature, your ideas may appear lofty, or too intuitive and not grounded in reality.

For Executors: You may not move fast enough for them and if the timing or situation doesn't feel right, you procrastinate on taking action.

For Influencers: Your big idea may not be in alignment with theirs and could cause friction on creating a shared vision.

For Strategic Thinkers: Because you think big, your ideas may come across as flaky and not grounded in practicality.

Something to consider: Your belief in humanity and what is possible may be seen by others as flaky or unrealistic. Consider using real-life examples as proof of what is possible.

WHAT WILL HELP OTHERS CONNECT WITH YOU

Questions to Connect

- Is there someone or something that might make this project even better?
- What does this remind you of?
- Do you see a connection between this and anything else you are working on?
- What is the bigger picture here?
- What needs to feel right for you to take action?

Tips for Connection

- People high in Connectedness have a unique procrastination point. If they don't feel the timing is right or the right people are involved, they will delay or avoid taking action.

- Ask them what they're passionate about and then help them find out how to connect with others who feel the same way. They always prefer collaboration over competition.

- *Word of caution:* Be careful not to isolate them, they need other people around them. Also, be careful not to think that they are - or worse, calling them - unrealistic. They want the best for the group at large, whether it's their family, an organization, or humanity as a whole. Finding ways to "bridge the gap" is what inspires them.

Monica P. California, USA

As a teacher, I am always trying to excite my students about learning how to design. The first day of class starts with the same message "You will learn how to integrate the tools acquired in the last four years of the major into engineering design. We will work individually and in teams and go through a lot of practice problems to ensure that you become confident with the material. We will experience some moments of frustration, there will be mistakes made but by supporting each other, we will be able to master the design skills and will successfully finish the course with the design of a complete treatment system. The final project will be completed in little pieces. I know that it sounds challenging, however, I am confident that each of you will succeed. We just must go one step at a time".

In short, this is my Developer talking. I often say: "If every day you put in little work and time, at the end of the journey you will look back and be happily surprised at how much you have grown."

My Developer can get on steroids when I am giving verbal or written feedback. The recipient of can get overwhelmed and think that I am not happy with their work because I am so invested in their growth and continue finding different areas or ways to make things better or to improve

Developer®

110

Communication for DEVELOPER®

> *Your communication style contributes consistent recognition of progress being made and your delivery is notably tranquil and patient.*

According to Gallup®: People exceptionally talented in the Developer theme recognize and cultivate the potential in others. They spot the signs of each small improvement and derive satisfaction from evidence of progress.

Celebrate:

- Your dedication to progress
- Your talent-spotting skills
- Your patience
- Your belief in the potential of others

Evaluate:

- Are we making progress?
- Is this worthy of my time?
- Is the other person interested in developing themselves?
- Am I pushing too hard?

WHAT WILL HELP YOU

How to recognize it: You inspire others by consistently mentioning and recognizing the growth you see in their performance, ability, or skills. You have a naturally positive way of speaking and notice even the small steps others are making in their own progress - intentionally pointing it out so they can see it, too. You are encouraging and enthusiastic and transmit this when you speak.

How it might frustrate others: Your ability to see potential in others may come across as setting expectations for them instead of with them. They may feel it as pressure instead of encouragement.
For Executors: Your focus on the growth of others could have those high in this domain feel you are prioritizing people over important deadlines.
For Influencers: While you believe everyone has potential, they will prefer to have the right, key people involved.
For Strategic Thinkers: Your desire for collaborative and emotional involvement could interfere with their planning processes.

Something to consider: You may find it difficult to give or receive negative feedback. Recognize that for growth to occur, people need positive as well as developmental feedback. Use your ability to identify progress and potential to offer constructive criticism rather than solely give praise.

WHAT WILL HELP OTHERS CONNECT WITH YOU

Questions to Connect

- How do you recognize progress?
- How do you recognize potential?
- What are you doing to nurture someone's development?
- What can you do to celebrate small successes?
- What does it take to be a good mentor?

Tips for Connection

- Make sure they have opportunities for their own development. Ask what they would like to learn or how they would like to grow.

- Recognize them for their accomplishments, both large and small. They will appreciate it and feel "seen".

- *Word of caution:* Be careful not to overlook them. While often tasked with mentoring or training others, they are often passed over or not considered for their own growth and development, leaving them feeling unseen and undervalued.

Bree T. Ohio, USA

Empathy is a funny talent when it comes to communication. On the surface, it seems that the two would go together seamlessly. In reality, though, the talent of empathy can take unexpected pathways.

For me, empathy shows up the strongest in my role as a wellness coach. Many of my clients come to me frustrated, unhappy, and wanting to look and feel better. Using empathy, I can see beyond their words and body language to the deeper well of emotion. With the use of reflections and questions, I am able to help them tap into that emotion to commit to their next right action.

But sometimes it takes an unexpected turn. Empathy can pick up on things that others aren't ready to admit or share. This can lead to a breakdown in communication when I push a conversation before the other person is ready. It's taken me years to learn that just because I can sense the emotion doesn't mean the other person wants to share.

For me, empathy and communication are like love and marriage. You can't have one without the other.

Empathy®

Communication for EMPATHY®

> *Your communication style contributes comfort with expressing your emotions often putting others at ease to express theirs.*

According to Gallup®: People exceptionally talented in the Empathy theme can sense other people's feelings by imagining themselves in others' lives or situations.

Celebrate:

- Feeling what others are feeling
- How you can "read a room"
- Expressing your emotions with ease
- Your kindness

Evaluate:

- Am I taking on the feelings of others too personally?
- Do I express my feelings adequately and appropriately?
- Am I being taken advantage of by others?
- Do I have clear boundaries?

WHAT WILL HELP YOU

How to recognize it: You easily give a voice to others who are less comfortable expressing their emotions. You pick up on the details and what's behind the words that are being said by others, discovering a deeper meaning to what they are saying. You express yourself through what you "feel" versus what you "think" and can translate the unspoken emotions in a room into something tangible to understand and act upon.

How it might frustrate others: Your desire to express your feelings may be interpreted as being too sensitive or too emotional.

For Executors: Your desire to explore how others feel about the plans or goals may feel like a detour from what actually needs to be done.

For Influencers: Your concern for others or your emotional expression may be considered misplaced or too specific and missing the broader impact of their vision.

For Strategic Thinkers: Your ability to sense their feelings may be seen as intrusive, especially when they aren't ready to share.

Something to consider: Because your emotional nature can be misinterpreted as being moody, overly sensitive, or even volatile, consider how to balance your ability to step in the shoes of others and express your own feelings without becoming too emotional to function.

116

WHAT WILL HELP OTHERS CONNECT WITH YOU

Questions to Connect

- How do you feel about it?
- Tell us who is not being represented well in this conversation.
- Who will be excited about this?
- Who won't be?
- What sentiments are you noticing that I'm missing?

Tips for Connection

- Give them space to express themselves. This balances their well-being and helps them feel heard and recognized.

- Ask them about what they are noticing around the general sentiments of others. This can help you see things from a perspective you may not have considered.

- *Word of caution:* Be cautious not to assume that because they can identify, and even feel, the feelings of others, means that they agree with them.

Karim G. Mexico

My Harmony theme plays a paramount role in my communication style. What I seek in my interactions is collaboration, so I ask myself: What is the best way I can say this message so we can avoid conflict and reach a (my) goal together? I can see this theme even in the moments most people lose their temper: I often need to call a bank call center, insurance company or my mobile phone service provider. These guys are receiving complaint after complaint all day long, so my communication style is always calm and open. I start by acknowledging the person's name, wishing a good day, and calmly communicating the issue. I rarely raise my voice, and I use the phrase "I know it is not your fault, but if someone can help me now it is you". I treat them with respect and kindness. Even if I get mad, I can raise my voice but never disrespect the person on the line. At the end of the call, I thank them by using their name. I rarely don't get what I need in just one phone call.

Harmony®

Communication for HARMONY®

Your communication style contributes tranquility and calmness to negotiate easily with all parties in order to establish a common ground.

According to Gallup®: People exceptionally talented in the Harmony theme look for consensus. They don't enjoy conflict; rather, they seek areas of agreement.

Celebrate:

- Your calm and balanced nature
- Your ability to gain consensus
- Seeing reciprocity as a win-win and it's not always 50/50
- Your negotiating skills

Evaluate:

- Am I avoiding conflict?
- Am I just 'people pleasing'?
- Am I being truthful or evasive to keep the peace?

WHAT WILL HELP YOU

How to recognize it: You are an expert negotiator and mediator. You will always put a voice to the common ground to bring people together and show them that working together is the best way to accomplish what we desire. You tend to speak calmly - or distract those involved from the conflict - in order to ease tensions that may have arisen. You are very good at expressing the viewpoints of others to alleviate misunderstandings.

How it might frustrate others: Others may see you as wishy-washy and unable to make a decision if you're trying to make all parties happy - or perhaps you minimize the importance of the debate.
For Executors: Your keen awareness of the rough waters ahead may try to derail the current tactics of what is trying to be achieved.
For Influencers: With your ability to see problems or conflicts arising, you may try to keep them from expressing themselves the way they want.
For Strategic Thinkers: When you minimize the debate, it feels as if you are cutting them off from more deeply understanding what is happening.

Something to consider: Even though your natural reaction to a conflict may be to immediately cave in or avoid it altogether, use the friction to find a productive middle ground that uses the best of every perspective. Help the group stay focused on the common ground, bringing to mind the practical aspects of the situation, and influence the outcome as only you can.

WHAT WILL HELP OTHERS CONNECT WITH YOU

Questions to Connect

- How do you think we could bring people together?
- Where's the discord?
- Where are things working really well or in balance?
- Who do you work best with?
- What needs to be fine-tuned?

Tips for Connection

- Ask them if they are noticing unresolved or silent conflicts that may be causing issues - they can lend a different perspective to what is seen on the surface.

- They are open to debate, but appreciate it when things can be discussed peacefully and all parties are considered.

- *Word of caution:* Because they may put their head in the sand in certain situations - all in the name of keeping the peace - it may take others by surprise when they finally do face the situation, causing others to see them as hypocritical or contradictory to their original position

Michele K. Delaware, USA

How do you tell a full story? By listening to many perspectives. My Includer always wants to understand what voices aren't at the table and see if I can bring justice to that voice in the platforms where I get to share. I can speak from my self-opinion but sharing that my perspective is informed or sharing other perspectives I've sought out shows that my contribution may be of my own, but is not limited to just me.

As an educator, it's important that I bring the student voice to the table in addition to my expertise. By seeking out students whose perspectives differ from my own, my expertise is broadened and better informed.

Includer®

Communication for INCLUDER®

Your communication style contributes a kind and collaborative tone, which lends itself to being a voice for others who may not be heard.

According to Gallup®: People exceptionally talented in the Includer theme accept others. They show awareness of those who feel left out and make an effort to include

Celebrate:

- Your abilities as a natural team builder
- Making others feel at ease, especially new people
- Your acceptance of others as they are
- How you fight for or support the underdog

Evaluate:

- Am I being indecisive?
- Am I avoiding confrontation?
- Am I including the *right* people for the task at hand?
- Am I being overly generous?

WHAT WILL HELP YOU

How to recognize it: You often ask who isn't in the room and why. You desire to bring people together, asking questions that find commonalities to demonstrate that differences are what make us stronger. You invite others to participate by asking questions to get to know them or by simply bringing them into the conversation. You celebrate diversity and welcome different viewpoints as it better informs you and can lead to more creative and collaborative solutions.

How it might frustrate others: Your desire to include everyone may frustrate others who prefer a more intimate gathering.
For Executors: "Too many cooks spoil the pot." Your need to make sure everyone is contributing may be seen as prohibitive to a productive outcome.
For Influencers: Your need to hear all opinions and to have everyone's buy-in may delay the process of moving a vision forward.
For Strategic Thinkers: Your desire to bring more voices to the table may cause them to feel that their solitary thinking space has been invaded.

Something to consider: You may inadvertently invite others to join when the others involved might prefer to keep a tighter circle. Recognize your natural tendency to bring everyone in is not always ideal, and learn to put it aside when fewer players are the way to go.

WHAT WILL HELP OTHERS CONNECT WITH YOU

Questions to Connect

- Who's missing?
- How do you reach out to people that are seen as outsiders by others?
- How do you enjoy making new people feel welcome?
- Who do you need to bring on board?
- Who would be a dream partner?

Tips for Connection

- Ask for their opinion and input - especially what they have heard from others. They tend to form their opinions with a collective voice.

- Give them space to be vulnerable and be heard. They appreciate having their own voice heard as well.

- *Word of caution:* While they may often be the ones doing the inviting, remember to reach out to them once in a while and make sure they feel valued as well. Always being the proactive one can have them feeling lonely if they aren't included as well.

Marina M. California, USA

Leading with #1 Individualization, one of my top strengths is being a great "Story – Listener." I love listening and asking personalized follow-up questions to deepen my understanding of others. I intuitively spot and understand their inner motivations, talents, and intrinsic way of approaching life. When communicating with me, others feel heard, safe, and understood, and it helps us to create a foundation for authentic communication and trust. There is a "Chameleon Effect" in my communication with others because I use different words, rhythm, and conversational flow based on each person's needs, preferences, and communication styles. When I work with clients and as a manager, I notice how often and in what way every person likes me to check in with them and what kind of praise they prefer. I also help them communicate their strengths and personal preferences in areas like building relationships and learning experiences.

Individualization®

Communication for INDIVIDUALIZATION®

Your communication style contributes flexibility and creativity in the way you speak, meeting people where they are, and by speaking in a tone or manner they will understand.

According to Gallup®: People exceptionally talented in the Individualization theme are intrigued with the unique qualities of each person. They have a gift for figuring out how different people can work together productively

Celebrate:

- You celebrate the unique individuality and differences of each person
- How you make others feel special
- Recognizing all the factors which create the 'whole' person
- Your personalized attention

Evaluate:

- Is the group being sacrificed for the individual?
- Am I valuing potential over performance?
- Are the rules too flexible?
- Am I being too flexible – bending to the desires/needs of others?

WHAT WILL HELP YOU

How to recognize it: You are a communication chameleon. You notice details about people that most will miss. This helps you modify your tone, gestures, formality, etc in order to connect on a deeper level. You naturally tailor your message and delivery for your audience. You are likely to help point out the value that someone brings to a project or role, especially if you feel they are being overlooked.

How it might frustrate others: Your desire to "people-please" may actually be seen as disingenuous and superficial.

For Executors: By ensuring that each person has a chance to contribute according to their abilities you might be perceived as delaying progress.

For Influencers: As you are frequently focused on individual contributions, you may miss the bigger picture.

For Strategic Thinkers: You might be considered a roadblock when a one-size-fits-all approach or plan is necessary to make headway.

Something to consider: Your ability to shift communication styles with such fluidity could have others confused about your intentions or questioning your sincerity. Be sure to demonstrate your own authenticity by sharing vulnerably.

WHAT WILL HELP OTHERS CONNECT WITH YOU

Questions to Connect

- How can you make your contribution unique?
- What are the unique characteristics of this person?
- How can you personalize your goal and way of communicating?
- Do you find yourself picking out "just the right gift" for others?
- What stands out to you about this person?

Tips for Connection

- Recognize - and leverage them - for their personal contributions and unique gifts. They need this as much as they like to give it.
- Ask them what works for them and find ways to compromise if possible.
- *Word of caution:* Authenticity is key for them, they will spot "fake" personalities a mile away and appreciate true vulnerability as it deepens the connection and understanding they have with others.

Jennifer V. Colorado, USA

As a person high in Positivity, I talk about what's right, what's hopeful, and always focus on the glass being half full. Someone close to me recently said, "You're always focusing on what's good, but I'm more 'realistic'" I have the sense not to say what I'm thinking out loud, "Better to have loved and lost than never to have loved..." but I'm definitely thinking them.

I naturally get excited about things I experience and tell people about them. When I go to a good restaurant I rave about it to others. "You have to try it! It's SO good!" They often wonder, "Do you own it?" "No," I say, "I just loved it!"

I'm the first to praise. I value words of encouragement. I'm always looking at the bright side.

My teenager recently called me out on my positivity. Whenever she says anything that feels negative to me or critical to someone else, I point out the positive. If she says, "That person was really rude to me today!" I reply with "Maybe they just had a hard day. I'm sure they didn't mean it." She turned it around on me.

"You try it. Tell me something hard about your day. And I'll be you."

"I had to get up really early this morning to teach a class and I'm exhausted," I said.

"At least you got to see the sunrise!" she replied.

"You're right, that is annoying!"

Positivity®

Communication for POSITIVITY®

> *Your communication style contributes obvious energy, enthusiasm, and an ability to encourage others in challenging circumstances.*

According to Gallup®: People exceptionally talented in the Positivity theme have contagious enthusiasm. They are upbeat and can get others excited about what they are going to do.

Celebrate:

- Your 'silver-lining' attitude
- The ability to visualize a positive outcome
- Your abundance of gratitude and compliments
- Your infectious smile

Evaluate:

- Am I avoiding problems?
- Am I being naive?
- Am I complimenting with sincerity?
- Am I actively seeking positive outcomes?

WHAT WILL HELP YOU

How to recognize it: You have the ability to lift others quickly, even when they are in a bad mood. With your contagious energy and enthusiasm, you inspire, motivate, and help create an environment in which great collaborations thrive. You are a natural cheerleader, keeping others moving forward. You give compliments easily and your carefully selected praise is at the center of how you recognize the contributions of others.

How it might frustrate others: Your need to find the silver-lining or the "blessing in the lesson" can have others feeling dismissed or frustrated as their current emotional state is diminished.
For Executors: Your positive outlook may be thought of as unrealistic and not taking the appropriate actions necessary to accomplish the task at hand.
For Influencers: Your immediate optimism may be seen as overshadowing their assessment of a situation, threatening their autonomy to act as they see fit.
For Strategic Thinkers: Your perky nature may rub them the wrong way when serious planning or problem-solving is happening.

Something to consider: Be cautious not to force or overplay your cheerful energy. People are overly cautious of people who always put on a good face and may disregard your judgment as too starry-eyed, so channel your positive energy in actionable ways to influence others.

WHAT WILL HELP OTHERS CONNECT WITH YOU

Questions to Connect

- Which types of people excite you?
- What is usually the best thing about your conversations?
- What do you need to remain positive?
- What are the possible solutions you see?
- What's your favorite thing to notice about others?

Tips for Connection

- Lean into their optimism, especially when you are having a hard time seeing the "silver-lining".

- Remember to pay them sincere, small compliments or recognize them for something they have contributed. They will deeply appreciate it and it will boost their connection and trust with you.

- *Word of caution:* Even people with high Positivity can have down days. They need a chance to feel the "feels" and won't appreciate being cheered up too quickly. Give them a little space, they know better than almost anyone that there is light at the end of the tunnel.

Susan C. California, USA

I have always enjoyed meaningful and engaging 1:1 conversations both at work and in my personal life with people to who I feel authentically connected. When I meet someone for the first time, I quickly determine if the person is genuine and open to having transparent conversations. If that trust and rapport is there, I can easily delve into deeply personal and even controversial topics. On the flip side, if I sense that someone is engaging on a superficial level or not revealing their true nature, I am much more guarded and private. This results in having a few long-term friendships and people who I can talk to about anything at any time. However, with people who I have not established that level of genuine and authentic communication with, I come across as private and difficult to get to know.

Relator®

Communication for RELATOR®

> *Your communication style contributes genuine and authentic connection through deep and empathetic conversation.*

According to Gallup®: People exceptionally talented in the Relator theme enjoy close relationships with others. They find deep satisfaction in working hard with friends to achieve a goal.

Celebrate:

- Your loyalty and trustworthiness
- Your values of honesty and authenticity
- Your close circle of friends
- How easily you build relationships

Evaluate:

- Am I isolating people?
- Do I appear closed off or aloof?
- Do I play favorites?
- Am I holding any grudges?

WHAT WILL HELP YOU

How to recognize it: As a person who profoundly values loyalty and confidentiality, you usually prefer one-on-one communication over speaking in larger groups. You build rapport through genuine, empathic conversations which lead to long-term friendships or partnerships. People easily trust you because of your authentic nature, though you may be slow to trust others.

How it might frustrate others: Because of your tight circles, you may appear unapproachable to others, and they may see you as having "favorites".
For Executors: Your need to connect and converse may throw them when all they want to do is to get to the point and move on.
For Influencers: Your small circles may feel limited when spreading the message and getting buy in from others.
For Strategic Thinkers: You may find it difficult to open up and share in conversations and plans if you aren't already feeling some level of trust with them, causing them to question your commitment or interest.

Something to consider: Because you're drawn to people with whom you've already established trust, be aware that you may appear to others as cliquish. Be sure to include others, especially when delegating, and give people a chance to win your trust as well.

WHAT WILL HELP OTHERS CONNECT WITH YOU

Questions to Connect

- Is your inner circle small but mighty?
- Which relationships can you draw on to help you achieve your more urgent goals?
- How can you get to know the people around you better?
- Do you have a close group of friends or family members you can count on?
- Who are the most important people around you?

Tips for Connection

- Engage them in conversation before getting to the point. Ask them how they are doing or even better ask them about something they care about like their family or a hobby.

- Be present when talking with them No checking emails or your phone. They want to know you are fully engaged and this helps establish trust.

- *Word of caution:* Be sure not to isolate those with this talent. They need their people around them, even if it's just sitting in silence.

STRATEGIC THINKING

The mind is not a vessel to be filled, but
a fire to be kindled.

Plutarch

Strategic Thinking

According to Gallup: Those who are able to keep people focused on "what they could" be are constantly pulling a team and its members into the future. They continually absorb and analyze information and help the team make better decisions.

Talents in this Domain

**Analytical   Context   Futuristic   Ideation
Input   Intellection   Learner   Strategic**

Do you know someone high in Strategic Thinking talents? You know, the Thinkers & Philosophers? The ones who believe that thinking IS taking action? Did you know they have a certain communication style?

Those who are high in Strategic Thinking talents love the details, the more the better for them. It's important to have all the information so they can understand the situation and minimize risk to find the best possible solution. They tend to ask a lot of questions - it's not an interrogation, though it may sometimes feel like it. It's their genuine curiosity and a deep need to have all the facts. Being wrong is not something they take lightly - avoiding mistakes is their MO.

Be prepared with proof when speaking with those high in this talent area. And don't misinterpret their groundedness in reality as a lack of emotion. For them, there is a time and place for both.

Typical Characteristics

- Persistent and steady
- Consistently monitors & confirms status of plans
- Problem solver
- Keeps focused on what could be
- Stretches others' thinking for the future
- Constantly absorbing and analyzing information
- Helps people make better decisions

Communication Style

- In general, wants details
- Minimizes risks and dislikes surprises
- Needs time to be comfortable with the plan
- Situation and find the facts
- Spends time clarifying problems and issues
- Anchor of reality
- Thorough and a good planner

Things They Might Say or Do

- What are the possibilities here?
- How did we get here?
- What's the plan?
- What are you thinking?
- Likely to be quiet at meetings
- Might ask for more details than are available – or necessary
- Might ask "why not" more often than "why"
- Might appear cold (lacking emotion)
- Might sit apart from the group or claim more personal space than others

Rhonda M. Oklahoma, USA

I find my Analytical strength working overtime when I communicate in a new relationship. Whether it be a new co-worker or prospective friend, I like to gather information in order to analyze how (or if) the relationship might progress. I ask questions, watch for behavior cues, listen for tone, and assess the environment to formulate opinions on the new person in my life.

Until I have this data, and the opinions formed from it, I lack the comfort and motivation to move forward. I'm a little impatient, and a quick study, so I tend to want a lot of information quickly. For the betterment of all, I must balance my desire for it with a more organic approach to relationships.

In established relationships, Analytical comes to the forefront when discussing new goals. How do we want to get this done? Let's talk through some options so I have something with which to work. I'll analyze the options and move forward with the one that makes the most sense!

Analytical®

Communication for ANALYTICAL®

> *Your communication style contributes a needed objectivity and level-headed approach, especially when emotions are running high.*

According to Gallup®: People exceptionally talented in the Analytical theme search for reasons and causes. They have the ability to think about all of the factors that might affect a situation.

Celebrate:

- Your desire for the truth
- Your ability to ask the 'right' questions
- Your methodical decision-making process
- Your cool head in tough situations

Evaluate:

- Am I stuck in analysis paralysis?
- Am I more worried about being right than finding compromise?
- Am I considering the emotional impact – on myself and others?
- Are all these questions necessary?

WHAT WILL HELP YOU

How to recognize it: In emotional settings, you offer an impartial approach, using data and analysis to move things forward and lower the heat of the situation. You tend to ask a lot of questions, searching for the proof you need to make the best decision possible. You can usually walk others through how you came to a decision because of your methodical approach to decision-making.

How it might frustrate others: Your need for data and statistics may come across as an interrogation, instead of being seen as your need to feel fully informed and make better decisions.

For Executors: While they will appreciate your attention to detail, they may feel "enough is enough" at some point and prefer to start taking action.

For Influencers: If you don't bottom-line the decision, they may tune you out and move on with or without the information necessary.

For Relationship Builders: Your more neutral approach may come across as uncaring or distant to those who prefer more "feeling" in their connections.

Something to Consider: Your analytical approach may sometimes come across as criticism or interrogation. Temper comments by keeping in mind the human factor of the group, the context, and the mood. Take cues from the feelings of others.

WHAT WILL HELP OTHERS CONNECT WITH YOU

Questions to Connect

- What additional data/info do you need to make a decision?
- Where can you go to get more data/info?
- What sticks out to you as being important here?
- What kind of proof do you need?
- What are your favorite sources of data to support your case?

Tips for Connection

- Ask targeted questions to open the true potential of their objective and multi-factor mindset. This will help balance facts with feelings and perceptions with reality.
- When entering a conversation, be prepared to offer a few facts or "proof" of your observations, especially when problem-solving or discussing difficult situations.
- *Word of caution:* Be prepared to give them the data or information they are missing, but recognize that while they need it to make a decision, they may not know where to go or whom to ask for it.

Maghan H. New York, USA

"You're such a linear thinker." An old boss once jokingly said this to me after I spent a few minutes summarizing the events leading up to wherever we were at that moment in time. The comment has stuck with me for years not just because I took it as a dig at my slower approach but also because it's simply not true. It's not my *thinking* that's linear but my communication style.

It's my Context (#4) that helps me communicate the often-interconnected web of ideas, patterns, and relationships. My Connectedness (#3) is constantly sensing in the information I'm taking in with my Learner (#1) & Empathy (#2). Communicating based on date or sequence provides a pathway for me to sort and organize what might otherwise come out as a jumbled mess.

And since I lean heavily in Relationship Building talents, Context also serves as a way to show care, communicating that I've heard what someone has shared and am taking it into account. Now I tell co-workers that context is my love language — it's how I communicate and how I appreciate others communicating with me.

Context®

146

Communication for CONTEXT®

Your communication style contributes questions and insights that draw a thread through where we come from and aim it to where we are going.

According to Gallup®: People exceptionally talented in the Context theme enjoy thinking about the past. They understand the present by researching its history.

Celebrate:

- That you have a relevant, historical perspective
- Your love for the backstory
- Learning from past mistakes
- Respecting your predecessors or elders

Evaluate:

- Am I too focused on the past?
- Am I holding a grudge?
- Questioning the perspectives without trust?
- Am I resisting change?

WHAT WILL HELP YOU

How to recognize it: You love to connect through backstory - your own, someone else's, or information needed behind a current situation. You prefer to make decisions when you have a full panorama of the situation. You are a natural record keeper and scrapbooker. You have a natural power to connect the past & the present which can lead to better solutions or plans for the future.

How it might frustrate others: Your need to understand the root of a problem or situation might make others feel like you are unable to move on from the past.

For Executors: Your need to know where we've been or what led us to this point, may be of little interest to those who are taking actions for today and tomorrow.

For Influencers: Your affinity for memories and how things were, can feel like an impediment to the grander vision moving forward.

For Relationship Builders: Your deep connection to past events may be seen as holding a grudge or an inability to move toward building a new relationship.

Something to consider: You may be perceived as stuck in the past and without a vision for tomorrow if you always need to start with what has already happened. Use your knowledge appropriately to share relevant history and background while expressing your desire to create a better outcome in the future.

WHAT WILL HELP OTHERS CONNECT WITH YOU

Questions to Connect

- What does your experience tell you?
- What is one of your favorite memories?
- What can we learn/have you learned from the past?
- Tell me about a similar experience from your past.
- Tell me about a time when...

Tips for Connection

- Allow space for questions around background and what has happened before. This will help them make better decisions and move forward more confidently.

- Consider them for projects or tasks which require investigative research, they will enjoy it more than most.

- *Word of caution:* They might appear resistant to big decisions or actions being taken if they feel that past mistakes are being repeated or there is no historical consideration as to the future outcome. They will want to offer a counter option to ensure better results based on what they have learned from the past.

Aaron V. California, USA

Having Futuristic as a top strength is a blessing and a curse. It is dreaming about 'what could be', but waking up to 'what is'." As a Futuristic, being surrounded by process-oriented people who also keep the end goal in mind is critical to getting the most out of someone who has this talent as a top skill. Meetings and conversations that are vision-orientated and spark imagination of the life or future that could be lived are where I feel something ignite within me. It makes me want to contribute my best efforts & talents as a vision comes to fruition.

The caveat in how this might frustrate others is that I tend to be seen as "not in the present". Being someone who is inspired by the future lends itself to be viewed as not focused on what is front of me. If you work with someone who is Futuristic and can relate to this experience, I encourage you to have them articulate the plan they have in place for achieving their vision and put them in the company of trailblazers.

Futuristic®

Communication for FUTURISTIC®

> *Your communication style contributes inspiration and vision, always exploring "What if?" and "What could be".*

According to Gallup®: People exceptionally talented in the Futuristic theme are inspired by the future and what could be. They energize others with their visions of the future.

Celebrate:

- Your creativity and imagination
- Your vision for a better tomorrow
- The ability to see possibility instead of roadblocks
- Your ability to dream big

Evaluate:

- Am I appreciating the here and now?
- Am I being realistic with my vision of the future?
- Am I remembering to say thank you or appreciate current efforts?
- Am I co-creating with others or am I telling others how it should be?

WHAT WILL HELP YOU

How to recognize it: When you consider the future, you generally come from one of two perspectives. You either ask, "what if...?" or you may focus more on how to avoid what's coming. Your imagination and desire to innovate drive you to inspire others to create a new or better way to move forward. You speak of potential and possibility, recognizing the opportunities to create growth and improvement.

How it might frustrate others: You may be thinking so far in the future that others can't keep up.
For Executors: Your dreams and visions may be seen as added weight to their to-do list, not realizing you are just exploring possibilities.
For Influencers: Your dreams may be seen as so big, they need to bring you back to the current vision in order to keep others motivated.
For Relationship Builders: You may be perceived as not being fully present and always wondering where things are going versus enjoying where we are.

Something to consider: You may be challenging to understand because your Futuristic ideas are, inherently, abstract. Concrete thinkers need something more visible to hold onto. Use your vision to inspire conversations -- through analogies, examples, stories, and parallels - and to help others see what you see.

WHAT WILL HELP OTHERS CONNECT WITH YOU

Questions to Connect

- What are your long-term goals?
- What kind of vision could you give us for this goal?
- How do you see this playing out?
- What do you see happening as a result of ...?
- What excites you about the future?

Tips for Connection

- Recognize the dream or vision before you start poking holes in their ideas.
- Give them space to dream and consider all the possibilities - either alone or with others. Great ideas can come from unexpected places sometimes.
- *Word of caution:* Keep in mind *how* they see the future. Some people worry about what is coming and look for ways to prevent it. Others see possibility and prefer to focus on expansion and innovation. Both have their value.

Sāska W. Netherlands

When my daughter Alisja was around 8 years old, she would not always have the patience to learn for her tests, especially those of less interesting subjects. So I needed to find a playful way to help her with it. I would ask her questions or read bits of text she needed to memorize by pretending to be someone else. I used different accents for my acting parts. Sometimes I would be a serious British news journalist, other times I would be a Big Bird from Sesame Street. She would happily give the answers in the same way. This made learning a lot of fun. Alisja would not only remember the facts she had to learn, but she would also remember which character owned a particular piece of information. Even now, years later, we still laugh about this creative method I came up with.

Ideation®

Communication for IDEATION®

Your communication style contributes quick thinking, fresh perspectives, and a desire to share all ideas - good and bad - because you never know where the inspiration will be born.

According to Gallup®: People exceptionally talented in the Ideation theme are fascinated by ideas. They are able to find connections between seemingly disparate phenomena.

Celebrate:

- Your love of brainstorming
- Making connections others may overlook
- Your ability to innovate
- Asking "why not?" instead of "why?"

Evaluate:

- Are my ideas actionable?
- Do I change direction too fast?
- Am I delaying the end goal?
- Am I communicating my ideas effectively?

WHAT WILL HELP YOU

How to recognize it: You rarely look for obvious answers when searching for a solution. You love to dive into your creative well to come up with novel and unexpected approaches, which in turn, inspire others and contribute toward finding solutions, new strategies, and new collaborations that work toward a common goal. You speak quickly so as to get all your ideas out and not lose your train of thought.

How it might frustrate others: You may overwhelm or confuse others due to your ability to see connections others don't and your rapid-fire delivery of ideas.
For Executors: If they don't know you're just thinking out loud, they will feel overwhelmed with the number of ideas they have to make a reality.
For Influencers: The number of ideas you can quickly churn out may be seen as derailing them or shifting them from the overall plan.
For Relationship Builders: Your random interjections of stories may have them feeling as if you're not listening versus your true intention to connect through a shared, though seemingly unrelated point in common - even though you easily see the connection.

Something to consider: Because you quickly see unseen connections and out-of-the-box solutions, be sure to speak your peer's language and stay on their wavelength to avoid confusion. Find a partner or partners with whom you can brainstorm and evaluate the best ideas going forward.

WHAT WILL HELP OTHERS CONNECT WITH YOU

Questions to Connect

- We need a fresh angle, can you help us see this differently?
- Ready to brainstorm?
- What ideas do you have around...?
- Does this feel like a fresh idea or a stale idea?
- What connections are we missing?

Tips for Connection

- Give them space to brain dump. There are no bad ideas for them and they need the chance to explore and filter to find the best ideas.

- Show interest in their ideas and ask them questions on how they came up with their solution. They may not always be able to explain the path, but if asked, it will help them verbalize the process more effectively.

- *Word of caution:* Before poking holes in their ideas, be sure to recognize their creativity and the possibilities they see. They know not every idea is a good one, but will get quite discouraged if their process isn't validated.

Jennifer R. Illinois, USA

I have always been a "collector" of information. Many people call this research. My INPUT is almost always "on". Whether I'm researching for a new home improvement project or learning more about my favorite hobby – gardening.

Professionally, my Input has helped me become an exceptional consultant. In Learning & Development and Organizational Change Management, initial research and analysis are critical to understanding the client's need so the right solution can be delivered. I collect information from interviews, meetings, resources, and intuitively through observation. This allows me to "see" a solution when others are still trying to figure things out.

Today I use two frameworks to help structure my communication, especially with the amount of information my INPUT collects. They are:

WHAT – SO WHAT – NOW WHAT

and **WHY – WHAT – HOW**

In a world where information is abundant, but where time is not, having a structure helps me communicate what my INPUT has helped me to understand, especially for my client's benefit.

Input®

Communication for INPUT®

> *Your communication style contributes an obvious wealth of information and resources that you are eager to share.*

According to Gallup®: People exceptionally talented in the Input theme have a need to collect and archive. They may accumulate information, ideas, artifacts or even relationships.

Celebrate:

- Your resourcefulness
- Your desire to share information & resources
- Having the right information, at the right time, for the right person
- Your better than average memory

Evaluate:

- Am I asking too many questions?
- Am I applying what I'm learning?
- Am I collecting things which have a purpose?
- Am I oversharing information?

WHAT WILL HELP YOU

How to recognize it: You are a natural curator of information and resources - both tangible and intangible. If you don't have the information when someone asks you for it, you will find it and share it as soon as possible. While problem-solving, you love to investigate and see what's already out there, finding solutions that already exist or can be built upon. You have an excellent memory and can elaborate in great detail on many topics.

How it might frustrate others: You can easily overwhelm others with the amount of knowledge or resources you have.
For Executors: They don't need a rundown of all the possible resources you have, they just need what works here and now.
For Influencers: Your curiosity and need to explore may pull them off track from the bigger picture that's already in motion.
For Relationship Builders: Your need to explore and experience all that is out there may feel inconsiderate to those who connect through familiarity and what they know.

Something to consider: Understand others may feel overwhelmed with the information you collect or your tendency to share too much, so be wise about what you communicate to truly move the needle in key moments. Ask good questions about what is needed and be focused on how and what you convey.

WHAT WILL HELP OTHERS CONNECT WITH YOU

Questions to Connect

- What resources do you already have that will help you with this situation?
- Where might you find the answer to that question?
- What info do you need to start moving forward?
- Have you shared this info with the necessary people?
- What's your favorite resource?

Tips for Connection

- Give them space for all their information and resources, whether physical or virtual. You may consider helping them to figure out how they want to organize as well but realize your way may not be their way.
- If you need someone to search for a solution or information, make them a priority, they love to know exactly how they can contribute.
- *Word of caution:* Be sure to give them opportunities to learn or explore. Repetition of tasks or one way of doing things will diminish their interest and productivity.

Ralph R. Switzerland

My experience with intellection: Why do I have to sprinkle my statements with "could be's" and "perhaps's" because, for me, it is absolutely obvious that nobody knows it all and that all interpretations are relative? I love this quote by Walt Whitman: "Do I contradict myself? Very well, then I contradict myself, I am large, I contain multitudes." What I believe about something can actually change within one conversation, and not even necessarily because of what you said, but because my mind always has multiple background processes running that make new connections and analyze things afresh.

Intellection®

Communication for INTELLECTION®

Your communication style contributes a thoughtful approach, generating new, complex, and valuable thoughts that inspire others, frame a course of action or set strategic direction.

According to Gallup®: People exceptionally talented in the Intellection theme are characterized by their intellectual activity. They are introspective and appreciate intellectual discussions.

Celebrate:

- Your depth and profoundness for understanding
- Your philosopher's mindset
- Having deep, meaningful conversations
- Your ability to move slowly

Evaluate:

- Am I isolating myself?
- Am I thinking about the right things?
- Am I getting frustrated with others who move faster than I do?
- Am I building walls or emotional barriers to keep others at arm's length?

WHAT WILL HELP YOU

How to recognize it: You are the philosopher. When you speak, you are thoughtful, measured, and have likely spent time pondering what exactly it is you want to say. While you may initially appear quiet, when you are interested in the subject matter, you can become quite verbose and ask lots of profound questions. Superficial conversation is of little interest to you, and being put on the spot to come up with an answer will make you uneasy.

How it might frustrate others: You may appear as being aloof and a loner due to your need for time and solitude to think and reflect.
For Executors: Your need to ask deep questions may seem a waste of time, disconnected from what really needs to happen.
For Influencers: Your constant questions may mean you feel like a challenge to motivate and bring on board with their vision.
For Relationship Builders: Your need for alone time can feel like rejection or an inability to share space and time with them.

Something to consider: Because you need solitary time for thinking, you may be perceived as a loner or standoffish. Let people know you need time to think before responding. Balance your inner reflection and your real-life strategy to guide thoughtful courses of action.

WHAT WILL HELP OTHERS CONNECT WITH YOU

Questions to Connect

- What do you think about this situation?
- What have you been thinking deeply about lately?
- How might it apply to this situation?
- Which of these ideas would you like to spend more time with?
- In what kinds of situations do you think best?

Tips for Connection

- Ask profound questions. They will appreciate the space to reflect and consider the deeper meaning and your interest in hearing their thoughts.
- Consider written communication, as this will give them time to think and formulate their response.
- *Word of caution:* Realize they need time to process. They will not be able to answer questions on the spot, even if that question is simple. Answers are not black and white for them and require time to respond appropriately.

Sally M. California, USA

My mind was blown when I went to the bottom of my "All 34 CliftonStrengths Report," and saw Communication #34. "How could this be? I TEACH a workshop on Communication Styles!" With the help of a coach, I discovered how we can overcome weaknesses by using our dominant talents.

Having low Communication talents means that sometimes I have a hard time putting thoughts into words. I need to think about what I want to say and how I want to say it ahead of time. To deliver effective workshops, I lean on my LEARNER to have deep knowledge about my topic (my INPUT #4 helps with this too). I know my materials really well so I'm comfortable presenting in front of people.

As a coach, I lean heavily on my LEARNER talents. I ask a lot of questions. I approach clients and new relationships with curiosity and let my LEARNER lead the way. In CliftonStrengths Workshops, I use my Communication #34 / Learner #1 combination to demonstrate how we can manage our "lesser talents" by leveraging our dominant ones. Just because COMMUNICATION is last on my list, it doesn't mean I can't communicate!

Learner®

Communication for LEARNER®

Your communication style contributes a natural curiosity about people and subjects, which leads to thoughtful questions and an open mind to new ways of doing things.

According to Gallup®: People exceptionally talented in the Learner theme have a great desire to learn and want to continuously improve. The process of learning, rather than the outcome, excites them.

Celebrate:

- Your curiosity about many things
- Your great perspective on a variety of subjects
- Your appreciation for different ways of learning
- Learning from your mistakes

Evaluate:

- Is this just curiosity or does it serve a purpose?
- Am I a know-it-all?
- Am I applying what I learn?
- Am I sharing and/or using my knowledge appropriately?

WHAT WILL HELP YOU

How to recognize it: Your natural curiosity allows you to form thoughtful and specific questions. You need to ask questions - for clarity, for deeper understanding, for your own personal satisfaction. You may also appear to be a perfectionist. If you feel you don't know enough to move forward, you won't move at all. You enjoy teaching, presenting, and explaining.

How it might frustrate others: Your need to ask a lot of questions may come across as either insecurity or unnecessary and intrusive.

For Executors: Your incessant questions may be considered an impediment to taking action and completing the task at hand.

For Influencers: Your constant need to know more may be perceived as going down the rabbit hole and thus, derailing the bigger vision and demotivating others along the way.

For Relationship Builders: The sheer number of questions can feel like an interrogation instead of curiosity and thereby seeing you as not respecting their boundaries and what they are willing to share.

Something to consider: Watch out for being perceived as a know-it-all and avoid drowning people with dry facts you have stored. Learn to read how people absorb information and leverage it to share your insights effectively with others and in a way that is meaningful to them.

WHAT WILL HELP OTHERS CONNECT WITH YOU

Questions to Connect

- Tell me about a new experience you have had or new information you have encountered.
- What did you discover in this experience?
- What do you need to learn to grow?
- Who has the information you need to complete this project?
- Where can you go to learn more?

Tips for Connection

- Be curious about them and what they are learning. They enjoy a chance to share and explain.
- Ask them what they would like to learn more about and give them the time, budget, and/or resources to dive in and study.
- *Word of caution:* Before assuming what they know, ask them, they may know more than you. And if you need an expert, they may be the person to tap. If they're interested in the subject matter, they'll dive in.

Lisa F. California, USA

My Strategic shows up as fast-paced communication. It's a theme that naturally skips ahead, determining where we are headed and the fastest way to get there. I can take in a lot of information and jump to conclusions about it quickly. This means that, as a listener, I sometimes have a tendency to anticipate what someone is about to say and how I'm going to respond – which is not really listening. When I speak I can often find the right words very quickly. But, with my mind already imagining a future endpoint, I may already be discussing concerns or benefits of what they are talking about – frustrating others who are talking about the present or immediate next steps.

I can compensate for poor listening or frustrating others by aiming my Strategic at the *purpose* of communication rather than the content. This theme enjoys that challenge: If, for example, the purpose is connecting, explaining, or inspiring, I can aim my Strategic at that purpose and communicate exceptionally successfully.

Strategic®

Communication for STRATEGIC®

> *Your communication style contributes enthusiastic energy and creative imagination, offering several options to find the best path to the desired outcome.*

According to Gallup®: People exceptionally talented in the Strategic theme create alternative ways to proceed. Faced with any given scenario, they can quickly spot the relevant patterns and issues.

Celebrate:

- How plan B is just the beginning for you
- You see patterns that others don't
- Your seemingly intuitive nature
- Your ability to see the "big picture"

Evaluate:

- Have I thought this through?
- Am I making the best choice?
- Am I considering others' opinions?
- Am I communicating my idea clearly?

WHAT WILL HELP YOU

How to recognize it: You speak quickly and anticipate what others will say with ease. You notice patterns in behaviors and words and will consolidate them into a singular idea. You start with the destination or outcome in mind. So, sometimes you think in reverse by first generating multiple alternatives to hit the objective.

How it might frustrate others: Your need for options can have you miss the simplest solutions or work overtime to get to them.

For Executors: You don't need to share all of your options, they prefer just the one they need to execute and move on.

For Influencers: Your lack of explanation about why you've come to your conclusions may not be persuasive or enable them to persuade others.

For Relationship Builders: Your need to plan and have options may be viewed as controlling the situation vs your desire to make everyone happy by offering choices.

Something to consider: Because you see things so intuitively, and process information so rapidly, you may assume people can see what you see and leave out key details for others. Be sure to take a moment and show them the path that got you to where you are.

WHAT WILL HELP OTHERS CONNECT WITH YOU

Questions to Connect

- What are the options?
- What are the possible outcomes?
- You're probably able to see some potential outcomes before the rest of us. Tell us what you see.
- Of all the options on the table, which appears best?
- What's the straightest line to the finish?

Tips for Connection

- Start with the desired outcome and then allow them to think outside the box to choose the best options. Allow them to ask questions for clarity to understand how to pick the path of least resistance to the goal.

- They will appreciate your trust in letting them design the best path to the goal - along with the flexibility to change paths if it becomes obvious it's not working

- *Word of caution:* They may not have a good poker face, so if you see their brow furrow, it may just be them processing the information and working through what they're going to say or do next.

Final Thoughts

I hope you have found the information included in this book useful to you. Regardless of our talents, we all communicate. With this book as a guide, I hope you discover new ways to connect with others and can now see them a bit more objectively.

Heck, it's my mission: *To live in a world where talents aren't wasted, potentials are realized, and happiness is contagious.* It's the backbone to everything I do, including - and most especially - this series of books.

If you are interested in deepening your knowledge through a strengths lens, please check out the page http://discoverjoself.com/practical-strengths-programs There you will find opportunities to deep dive into your own talents and grow with a group of peer mentors who are looking to do the same.

Other books in the Practical Strengths series, which are available on Amazon sites around the world:

- Parenting
  https://www.amazon.com/Practical-Strengths-Parenting-CliftonStrengths-Everyday/dp/B08XLGGFY8/
- Career Success
  https://www.amazon.com/Practical-Strengths-Success-CliftonStrengths-Everyday/dp/B09ZQ7V52K/

Coming Soon...
- Relationships
- Conflict Management
- Grief & Resilience
- Habits & Goal Setting
- Inner Compass
- Health & Wellness
- Recreation & Hobbies

If you'd like to be informed of new releases and occasional updates, as well as download strengths-specific resources and have the opportunity to be a part of the future books by sharing your own story, please visit:

http://discoverjoself.com/resources

About the Author

Jo Self is on a mission to teach CliftonStrengths® as a second Language. She seeks to create a world where everyone can live to their full potential, talents aren't wasted, and happiness is contagious. As a single mompreneur and expat - spending 11 years in Peru and recently relocated to Mexico - she understands the challenges and rewards that both entail. When she's not helping others create extraordinary lives, she can be found at the sewing machine, at the movies, enjoying a glass of wine with friends or horsing around with her terribly precocious little boy, affectionately known as O.

In the past, Jo developed nationally recognized and award-winning employee programs for Yum! Brands, the world's largest fast food restaurant company. And when she wasn't leading in-house teams to discover their strengths, she was on loan to other organizations helping them to do the same – all while serving on the national board of directors for her professional organization, ESM Association.

Once she left the corporate ranks, she started her own event business, Bon Vivant Savant, and was recognized as both a "Top Female Under 40" influencer in the community by Louisville Woman

Magazine and also as a leading entrepreneur in the "40 under 40" list by Business Week Magazine.

After leaving the States and moving to Peru in 2011, her entrepreneurial spirit continued with a tourism start-up that won a government grant as well as being recognized by ADEX as a top 50 start-up in the country. However, with all of these achievements, she still wasn't feeling fulfilled. A health scare in early 2015 set her on a course of self-reflection which brought her back to what she had always done best, had made her happy *and* given her joy. That answer was Strengths. She immediately contacted Gallup® and began the journey for what she now confirms is her true calling, being a Gallup® Certified Strengths Coach.

Embracing her own strengths-based life led to the creation of her course, The Language of You. She guides other coaches and heart-based entrepreneurs to align their mission with their message, connecting them to their ideal clients. She also works with larger organizations to improve communication, leading to higher engagement and better relationships among team members.

"It is my deep desire to share with the world the power and gift that the CliftonStrengths® language provides. It is the heart of this book series, Practical Strengths. I believe that sharing this language with one another leads to improving relationships through better communication and greater compassion for one another."

CONNECT WITH JO:

https://www.linkedin.com/in/joself/   http://discoverjoself.com

http://youtube.com/@discoverjoself

http://facebook.com/groups/speakingofstrengths

References

If you'd like to explore further:

Assessments

CliftonStrengths® for Students for ages 15-21
https://www.strengthsquest.com/

CliftonStrengths®
https://www.gallup.com/cliftonstrengths/

(I do not make any profit from sharing these links above)

Please visit http://discoverjoself.com/resources for more information on books and assessments along with my guidance for how to get the most out of the materials.

Made in the USA
Middletown, DE
25 October 2024

63270320R00104